P9-DEV-253

The Cats
of Moon Cottage

The Cats
of Moon Cottage

MARILYN EDWARDS

ILLUSTRATED BY
PETER WARNER

Hodder & Stoughton
LONDON SYDNEY AUCKLAND

First published in Great Britain in 2003

10 9 8 7 6 5 4 3 2

British Library Cataloguing in Publication Data
A record for this book is available from the British Library

ISBN 0 340 86206 8

Typeset in Goudy by Avon DataSet Ltd,
Bidford-on-Avon, Warwickshire

Printed and bound in Great Britain by
Clays Ltd, St Ives plc, Bungay, Suffolk

The paper used in this book is a natural recyclable product
made from wood grown in sustainable forests.
The hard coverboard is recycled.

Hodder & Stoughton
A Division of Hodder Headline Ltd
338 Euston Road
London NW1 3BH
www.madaboutbooks.com

For Michael,
who grins and bears it.

CHAPTER 1

This tale starts with an email. As emails go, this is not the most obviously momentous, but, put simply, it changed my life. It also had a marked effect on my husband, Michael, and his son John and, to a lesser extent, on his other two sons, Damian and Oliver. Here it is:

From:	Mitzi
To:	Broadcast everyone in office
Subject:	Kittens
Date:	22 May 1998 15:23

Our author, Susan Hill, has two seven-week-old kittens, one boy and one girl.

She's looking for a home for them, and would rather they stay together. If anybody's interested, please give Caroline a buzz.

From: Marilyn
To: Mitzi
Subject: RE: Kittens
Date: 22 May 1998 15:36

Mitzi, I have just talked to Michael and he says we can take them, which is wonderful. We have an old cat but I presume that won't be a problem. But of course someone might have got there first.
   Marilyn

From: Mitzi
To: Marilyn
Subject: RE: Kittens
Date: 22 May 1998 15:50

As far as I know, no one else has asked about them, so I think they're all yours. I'll let you know the details on Tuesday.

From:	Marilyn
To:	Michael
Subject:	FW: Kittens
Date:	22 May 1998 16:14

```
Hey, Michael - we are parents!
  Love M
```

From:	Michael
Sent:	22 May 1998 16:46
To:	Marilyn
Subject:	RE: Kittens

```
Now you can't shout at me for calling
you Mam!
  Hope Septi takes to them!
  Will you tell him or shall I?
```

And so it came to pass - well, nearly. But Michael's percipient question about Septi is to haunt me soon enough.

Meanwhile, back at the office, in the early evening of that same day, there is a sudden frenzy of activity as arrangements are made for a small drinks party to celebrate the engagement of one of our team to her young man. Just a quarter of an hour into the party, I'm unable to contain my excitement a second longer and find myself stepping forward. It is with only the smallest intent of wickedness, and with truly no aim of upstaging anyone – but more because my mind is full of whiskers and kittens – that I hear myself declaring loudly that Michael and I also have an announcement to make. Michael stares across the room at me, radiating apprehension, because he cannot second-guess what I am about to say and everyone falls disarmingly silent.

Now embarrassed, I raise my glass and mumble coyly: 'Michael and I would like to tell you all that we are about to become parents.' I will remember that silence for the rest of my life, heightened as it was by the exquisite expression of confusion and incredulity on the face of our boss. Pregnancies abound in our office, and while they are naturally supported, the ensuing need for maternity leave always creates a wake of problems. At fifty-plus years of age, I, and therefore Michael, had for some time been considered to be safely beyond all that sort of thing.

Shamefully unable to maintain the suspense any longer, I explain prosaically that this is more by way of an adoption, and a feline one at that, and with visible relief our boss rallies and offers us warm congratulations and all happiness with our new offspring.

CHAPTER 2

May 1998

On returning to our cottage in Hertfordshire that weekend, however, Michael and I seriously begin to contemplate how the resident aged cat, Septi, might react to a kitten in his life. It is now to be one kitten, not two; as the second one had already been given a home before my email reached Susan Hill.

By this time Septi, named in full 'September' after the month in which he was acquired, has been a member of Michael's household from his late kittenhood until the full maturity of his now seventeen years.

During those years he has endured many moves and tiresome disruptions to his fiercely guarded routines. He has survived any number of unintentional shutting-ins and shutting-outs, uncounted numbers of fights, several road accidents – of which one, certainly, would have killed any lesser cat – and has generally just been left to get on with it, through times of love and also of neglect. So Septi, now in his later years, has developed an independence and aloofness that Kipling would recognise immediately. He does indeed walk by himself on the 'wet wild roofs, waving his wild tail and walking by his wild lone'. In short, he is his own cat. He patrols his domain, the cottage, the garden and the immediate environs, with *brio* and immaculate attention to detail, which, among other things, entails seeing off no end of neighbouring cats.

Septi deserves a proper introduction. He is a neutered, male, short-haired, tabby moggy. Long bodied, he has ebony-dark shiny fur, which is exceptionally silky to the touch. He sports a smart white waistcoat and a full set of matching socks. Septi has a slightly haughty expression, and can look down his nose as no other cat of my acquaintance. He has a nick in one ear, acquired in a long-distant battle, magnificent fierce white whiskers, and penetrating large, greeny-brown eyes. He also has slightly broken, yellowing teeth but manages to eat perfectly well with them.

One unusual feature of Septi is his oddly strangulated voice. Miaowing, for him, always appears to take a considerable effort, and the sound that he emits suggests nothing less than that a pair of hands might be clamped around his throat. Notwithstanding that, he can yowl loudly enough to wake me, although not always Michael, when locked out in the rain in the yard under our bedroom window. But, and this is gloriously his, he has a mellifluous and deep purr, which he can sustain for astonishingly long periods. His purr is special; he can fill the whole cottage with it. It thrums through you. It is an operatic purr.

He is a loving cat, for all his aloofness, and bestows his affection on each household member in turn. When he is in the mood, he will especially seek out all three of the boys and, in particular, John. Who, precisely, in the family *is* his guardian continues to be robustly debated and remains unresolved. John thinks he probably took charge of Septi by default when he was still a small kitten. His brothers, Damian and Oliver, both wanted dogs and John was the only one who declared an interest in possessing a cat. Damian, on the other hand, believes that Septi was introduced as just the house cat, pure and simple.

In our household at the time that this story begins, John, of the three brothers, is the one who lives with us permanently; the other two make spasmodic weekend raids, and Damian is in fact currently domiciled in South Africa. Septi had, however, lived with Damian for six months, four or five years earlier, which seems to have resulted in mutual respect, as well as a reciprocal love.

What else about Septi?

He has a pronounced and morbid fear of thunderstorms, and if I know he is outside when a storm is brewing and I am not there to let him in, I become anxious on his behalf. As for finding himself near fireworks, he would rather be buried alive I believe. His one physical weakness, I sometimes think, is that a small lump on his back possibly hurts him, as I have noticed that occasionally, if he is stroked too firmly along his back, he will bite the hand that strokes, more warningly than penetratingly; but disconcerting for the stroker, nonetheless.

Over the span of his life, Septi has been a rapacious hunter and able to kill all manner of animals with quick efficiency, but by the time I entered his life, his hunting, for the most part, is over. There is an oft-repeated story of an occasion in his youth, when Michael's youngest son, Oliver, circa five years old, embarked upon an experiment with profound results. Early one morning when all other human members of the household were soundly asleep, the young boy, awake and bored, took it upon himself to entertain Septi by introducing him to his hamster. Oliver was in fact the proud owner of a pair of hamsters, but on this particular morning he restricted the formalities to just one of them. To his delight, the cat and the hamster had a most lively game together.

When John rose from his bed a short time later, however, he was saddened to find the small corpse of the very same hamster and a faraway look in Septi's eyes. Perhaps, in order to protect Oliver's sensibilities, not enough emphasis was laid upon the mortal dangers inherent in such play and, in the tradition of Greek tragedy, the following day the same terrible scene unfolded with the remaining hamster.

Septi never had it so good.

CHAPTER 3

June 1998

So now the moment has arrived.

'Will you tell him, or shall I?'

We both try. I open the batting.

'Septi, come over here. There's a good fellow. Look, there's something I need to say to you. I do know that just at the beginning, you will hate it and you will feel really iffy about it, but I promise you, it will be all right, really, eventually. Trust me.'

Michael watches this performance from me with an incredulous grin. He leans down and scoops Septi up in his arms, holding him close, and the great cat purr revs up, increasing in volume as Michael strokes him in all his favourite places. Septi rubs his cheek against Michael's and then glances across at me, down his nose, with an expression on his face that I cannot fail to interpret as 'eat your heart out'.

Michael murmurs into the top of his head almost, but not quite inaudibly: '*She* wants to bring a horrid little kitten into your life and ruin your peace and destroy everything that you are used to, and all that you enjoy most. So what do you think to that, boy? How does that grab you then?'

Out for a duck.

What is this male bonding stuff, this total resistance to change, I wonder crossly, but not without feeling a twinge of guilt. Michael winks at me and I flap a tea towel at him, in frustration. Septi continues to purr obliviously.

I hear myself pleading pathetically: 'Why don't you support me, Michael? If you don't help me with this, then I might just as well phone Susan Hill, now, and say it's off!'

Michael shrugs and observes: 'Don't think Septi really got what I said, anyway.'

'Yes, he did. I reckon he clocks much more than you think. There is an essence of understanding that I'm sure he has.'

'Don't think so, but all right. Listen, Septi. A kitten is coming and you will enjoy, OK? Acceptable, Marilyn? Does that fit the bill?'

Having exhausted the supply of tea towels, I stomp off upstairs and run myself a diverting bath. As I lie down in the water and watch it rise up the sides, I find myself smirking as I realise I'm taking part in the activity of displacement in more than just one sense.

5 June

At last the day I have been yearning for dawns and we are in Solihull for a meeting. This day was nominated as our day for collection as Solihull is close to the home of the kittens, but the waiting time has stretched out endlessly.

By mid-afternoon the meeting has drawn to a close and we are free to go in search of the longed-for kitten, and after a thirty-minute car journey we find the village. Michael navigates the car down a long winding driveway and we pass between several fields and beside a large pond and, finally, after several twists and turns we pull up in the yard and are greeted, with great warmth, by Susan Hill, who walks towards us, accompanied by a lean red and white shorthair cat. Having exchanged greetings with our hostess, Michael and I both bend down to say hello to this fit-looking feline, but in a very businesslike way and with no sign of embarrassment, the cat turns away, fully occupied with making her toilet in an old horse trough, now filled with soil. She completes her task and we are introduced. She is Tallulah, the mother of the kittens. I ask Susan who the father might be and she reckons that the dad is a regular consort from the nearby housing estate.

Susan invites us to follow her into a fine, rambling, limestone farmhouse and we find ourselves in a large light kitchen, which is magnificently dominated by a long wooden table. And there, on this table, is pure joy. Pure Joy is the most beautiful kitten in the world. Of course, Michael and I were bound to fall in love with the kitten whatever she looked like, but this kitten is breathtakingly lovely. What greets our eyes is a small curled-up fur-ball who, as we enter, looks up and presents to us a tiny triangular heart-shaped face, animated by two enormous, penetrating *amber* eyes, surrounded by fabulous almond-shaped, geisha-stripes and finished off with large pert ears. Her overall colouring is predominantly stripy grey and black and white, with ginger slashes, and could properly be described as 'torbie', being a dark tabby tortoiseshell colour. She stands up unsteadily, on extraordinarily long and elegant legs, and sashays towards us – and before she reaches us, we are goners. Hook, line and sinker.

I nervously ask if this is to be our kitten, for love at first sight is what has happened. Susan, smilingly, reassures us. This is indeed the sole remaining kitten. Someone, locally, took the other one.

Because the kitten has been part of Susan's household for so long, Susan warns us that she has been named already, as she could not remain anonymous for all that time. Susan looks across at me, and says, in a level tone: 'Her name is Ottoline.'

I gasp. 'You mean as in Morrell?'

Now, laughing, she nods emphatically.

I dare not look across at Michael, but as I hold my head down, in my mind's eye I see images of Lady Ottoline's fierce, determined chin and recall her legendary death from cancer of the jaw, which had always seemed so ironic. Immediately all manner of other non-sequiturs float through my head, her untiring courtship of the artistic glitterati of her day, her intense relationships and arguments with Bertrand Russell and Augustus John, and those endless soirees. She had, at one time, lived in and around Bedford Square, and I had left not only part of my soul there, but also a chunk of my heart, having, coincidentally, worked and played in that same square for many years.

Although anomalous to label a tiny fluff-ball with such a grave name, it has a curiously right feel to it.

Anyway it is a done deed. 'OK. Ottoline then,' I murmur compliantly.

CHAPTER 4

Having carefully placed our precious nine-week-old bundle into a carrying cage, which we jam, for safety, on to the back seat of the car, we set off down the long drive in the direction of home. As we call out our farewells to Susan, we make a promise that we will keep in touch with a kitten-progress report.

At first, from the back of the car, we hear a series of tiny miaows, but then, as we continue to ignore the pleas, the small noises steadfastly develop into a crescendo. It is hard to believe that such a tiny animal is capable of generating the ear-shattering cries that are now emanating from the Lady Ottoline. They are heartrending. I acknowledge my caddishness. I also cannot put out of my mind the thought that her mother will probably be experiencing a similar anguish. The look on Tallulah's face as we had bundled Ottoline into the cat carrier had not escaped me. But now, suddenly, there is silence; and soon we are on the motorway and the silence continues.

After a long but uneventful journey, we arrive home and carefully transfer the cage and its tiny occupant into the house. The front door of our ancient cottage opens straight into the low-beamed sitting room, which is where most of our lives are lived and where Septi reigns supreme. As we enter the room, with cat cage in hand, Septi, who has been asleep on his usual chair, stares across at us apprehensively, possibly speculating whether an impending visit to the vet, which he hates, is on the agenda. Why else the cat carrier?

At exactly this moment, from the depths of the cage, we all hear a small but distinct 'miaow'. Septi looks as if he has been electrified. On top of the aural assault, he has now picked up the feline scent. I cannot easily remember the last time I saw a cat with such a cross expression on its face. He looks furious. His mouth has pulled into that small governessy 'o' that cats effect so powerfully – his whisker pads are puffed out – and the tabby 'worry' lines above his eyes are even more drawn together. He is seriously put out and showing it.

We both feel concerned about letting the kitten out, but she has just endured a long and tiring journey and she really needs her freedom, and on the principle of 'in for a penny', we decide to release her and see what happens. Fumblingly, we open the cage door and one small, nervous kitten tumbles out into the room. Septi utters a deep growl of rage, glares at her, then quickly turns tail and runs from the room. Michael follows him and finds him by the back door, demanding to be let out. Septi's need to get away is so absolute that we have no option but to comply. Also, we are shocked by his growl; cats seldom growl, and it is always serious when they do.

Meanwhile, the innocent instigator of this agitation is busy investigating everything. Initially hesitant, her courage seems to increase by the second, and this small predatory creature, so recently torn away from her mother and uprooted from the only home she has ever known, quickly establishes her own familiarity with these new surroundings with growing confidence. We give her some Carnation Milk (Susan suggested this as being most like cats' milk), which she drinks, and soon she is eating a small mouthful of wet kitten food. We show her a cat-litter tray and wait; she uses it within half an hour of arriving. Ottoline has made a new home.

Meanwhile, we have the problem of Septi and his own concerns. A couple of weeks earlier I had taken Septi to the vet for the treatment of some minor ailment, but also to have him checked out, and he had been given a clean bill of health. But when I had asked my vet, a man in his sixties, on the brink of retirement and with all the experience that those years had yielded to him, what he thought might happen when I introduced a kitten into Septi's life, he had looked thoughtful and said:

'You do realise that this cat is a considerable age. And what you are doing is a major disruption to his well-organised life? He will accept it, or alternatively, I'm afraid, he might leave home. There is no knowing – it could go either way.' He then chuckled merrily: 'I'm darned certain that if it were me, *I* would leave home.'

I did not find this as amusing as he did, but laughed feebly all the same. Alarmed though I was at the time by this conjecture, on balance I reckoned that Septi liked his home comforts too much to do 'a runner', but I now recall this with increasing concern.

Eventually I manage to cajole Septi back into the cottage, and he enters with what seems to be an optimistic caution, hoping, perhaps, that the kitten has gone as rapidly as it had arrived. He walks, slowly, through the kitchen, towards the sitting room. The sight that greets him is an outrage. What he sees is one small kitten, who having made herself completely at home in the eating, drinking and cat-litter tray departments, is now snuggled up securely and comfortably on Michael's shoulder, as if she belongs there. He utters a long, low, guttural groan. So despairing, but also primeval, is this sound that it makes me worry and laugh all at the same time. Our immediate concerns are unfounded, in that no attack is forthcoming from Septi, although he is undoubtedly deeply unhappy. He lies stiffly and ill at ease on the edge of the sofa, sometimes staring at her, but mainly glaring morosely at the floor.

Suddenly Ottoline stirs herself from the reassuring warmth of Michael's shoulder, stretches her long elegant limbs in the manner of a completely mature cat, and jumps down on to the floor. She walks across the room until she is just under the cushion on which Septi is lying; she then lies down in an echo posture of his and looks coyly up at him. To begin with, he ignores her, then he stares down at her. She looks back at him very sweetly, at that moment oblivious to anything or anyone else.

And thus begins the beguiling of Septi.

Shortly after this first flirtatious endeavour by Ottoline, however, Septi firmly requests 'out' and spends the remaining part of the evening waving his wild tail on his wild own, somewhere in his private hiding places and when, finally, we do persuade him to come back inside the cottage, it is achieved only by the deceit of temporarily concealing Ottoline upstairs, where Septi tends to visit, rather than inhabit, so that he is persuaded that he has regained the mastery of his realm.

Within the confines of the cottage, Ottoline, during Septi's moody egress, has been displaying all her charms to us on full voltage and we have become completely captivated. She jumps from chair to desk and from desk to sofa; she runs with impeccable balance, as if it had been her lifelong habit, along the back of the sofa, and leaps fearlessly on to the mantelpiece. From there she springs straight on to another chair and up on to the high windowsill. She rests on her newly discovered ledge for a heady fifteen seconds, before descending into the first armchair and on to the floor. She then, languorously, rolls over on to her back and, revealing the soft snow-white fur of her belly, she daintily bends over the tips of each of her front paws and coquettishly tips her head on one side, assessing the effect of all this on her attendant audience with the one eye that is visible.

As Michael and I watch her admiringly, she changes her mood abruptly and springs up – first on to me and then on to Michael – brushes herself against our faces, and curls up on to our shoulders and then halfway round the back of our necks, that especial position seeming to be the most pleasing to her. She is wonderfully democratic with her favours, notwithstanding that each demonstration of affection never exceeds three minutes. John is away on holiday and, selfishly, in my infatuation, I'm grateful that on this first night I need only share her with Michael, although I am longing to see John's pleasure in her on his return.

By this time we have decided that Otto is the name. And Otto is what she becomes from now on. Otto the beautiful. Otto the brave. Otto the curious.

Having persuaded Septi to come back into the cottage, we find that Otto has, inevitably, emerged from her temporary concealment and followed us downstairs again where she continues with her all-important investigations of this new home. Septi, on seeing her, stalks off into the dining room. His mouth remains drawn together in that 'o'.

Reluctantly we tear ourselves away from the pleasures of kitten worship and prepare to head for the bedroom above. As we leave, we murmur gentle words of comfort to the old cat, stroking him lovingly but guiltily. We turn back and watch him walk, uncertainly, into the sitting room, his face bearing his newly permanent 'disgusted' expression. Finding a kitten-free zone, he curls up on the sofa, sighs deeply and buries his nose under his paw.

By the time we get upstairs, whence we have smuggled Otto, we have one very tired kitten on our hands and we place her carefully on the bed between us where she immediately falls soundly asleep, and so rests the household on this first night in Otto's new home.

CHAPTER 5

Andrew and Jane, much-loved stepchildren from my other family, are visiting England from their New Zealand home, and the following day come to stay with us for the weekend. They have shared their living with cats many times over and Jane, while watching Andrew manifestly falling in love with Otto, laughingly cautions us that there is no contest between a newly minted kitten and a mature old cat. I recognise the truth of this and make a silent vow to myself that we must take pains to prevent Septi from feeling eclipsed in any way by the feline usurper in our midst.

John returns from his holiday this same weekend and is bowled over by Otto as soon as he walks through the door. I watch his growing enchantment with the daft pride and pleasure of the newly besotted lover, but again become achingly aware that we must be mindful of Septi and his needs.

Meanwhile life continues and Michael, John and I all return to our respective jobs, leaving Septi and Otto to work out their *modus vivendi* in their own way. There is no cat flap on the cottage door and we have, until this time, let Septi out on demand. Otto is awaiting her injections against viral flu and feline leukaemia, so cannot yet be allowed out into the garden and beyond, and Septi seems to want to be out more than usual, so sometimes, when we leave for the office at our customary time of 6.50 a.m., he is out and resists all pleas to come back into the cottage. We are philosophical. It is summer and warm, and there is a shed and a greenhouse for him to shelter in if he needs protection from the sun or the rain.

From: Marilyn
To: Susan Hill
Subject: Ottoline and other things
Date: 11 June 1998 11:33

Dear Susan

It was really good to speak to you this morning. Please assure Clemency that Ottoline is well and happy and staggeringly bouncy and very much loved and cared for. I had to leave early last night in fact to take her to the vet for her jabs, and she was very brave and seems to have suffered no lasting side effects!! I was reassured too that you think Septi will come round - vet thinks so too.

I do feel for the sadness of her mum though - hope she recovers soon. If only one could reassure her that kitten is OK.

But thank you all for allowing such a wonderful bundle of joy into our lives - we are all soppy about her.

This email is generated by a phone call I had from

Susan, who explains that Tallulah, Otto's mum, has, contrary to their expectations, spent long hours repeatedly searching for her last remaining offspring who had been at her side until Michael and I came raiding, and that Clemency, Susan's resident daughter, is spending much time necessarily comforting her. I'm instantly mortified, of course, even though I know that someone, somewhere, would have had to have taken Otto away from her mum, had it not been us.

Before Michael and I started to share our life together, I had lived many years in the Yorkshire Dales, and had spent as many hours messing about playing at farming, outside normal working hours, as I was able to persuade the long-suffering local farmers to allow me. I kept my own flock of hens and I used to help at haytime and with milking, and also with calving, and sometimes sheep shearing, and always, when possible, lambing.

One of the annual rituals of sheep farming, however, against which I was never able to harden myself sufficiently, was 'spaining'. The ewes give birth to their lambs mainly through April, and even just into May in the Dales, and they live side by side contentedly enough

– apart, that is, from the repetitive, neurotic bleating of the ewes for their young to return to their sides. The greatest disruption to their daily tranquillity during this time comes in the form of being shepherded from one pasture to another, or even up on to the high hills, until the end of July. (At least, in normal years when the farms are not in thrall to the dreaded Foot and Mouth disease.)

Then one day in early August, triggered by the auction mart's calendar, it appears as if every Dales farmer who has any lambs at all decides that this is the week for spaining. This involves each individual farmer gathering up all of his sheep, and now substantially growing lambs, from his probably widely scattered pastures into one huge flock, separating out the lambs from the ewes, and containing the ewes in a field with fencing and a gate. The lambs are then removed to an equivalent pasture out of earshot of the ewes. This is a necessary exercise so that when the lambs go to market as 'store' lambs in the early autumn, they will have regained the weight that the trauma of separation will have caused them to lose, and the ones that are to go to market as 'fat' lambs will go within the next few days.

Because many different farmers will be doing this over a period of ten days or so, it means that the hills ring out, day and night, with the unceasing cries of ewes and lambs yearning to be with one another again. When it has been raining, if you go near the gate of spained ewes you will see by the churned-up mud exactly how many hundreds of times every single sheep has stamped back and forth, back and forth, at the gate where they last saw their young taken away. Many a Dales farmer finds it a difficult time too, and they will tell you that they know that the crying and the marching go on right through the night as well as during the daytime. The sound always brings tears to my eyes.

Tallulah, I salute thee and apologise.

A few weeks have passed and Otto has now received both lots of injections, and the time has come, we feel, to let her out into the garden. It is hard, too, domestically, keeping the back door shut through a warm summer. Septi has evidently become captivated by Otto, but we are yet to discover quite how much. He spends much of his time with her in the cottage, and I have found them both, upstairs on a sofa in John's room which gets the warm morning sun, fast asleep and clearly content in each other's company.

One fine Saturday morning in late June we let little, long-legged Otto out into the sunshine for the first time in her life and stand back to watch. She is fearful at the very beginning, as the sounds alone must be truly shocking to her 'protected' indoor ears, and she runs out and then runs back indoors again very fast. Finding the back door remains open she cautiously ventures out, but this time she stops, and looks about her with intense curiosity and starts, slowly, tentatively, to walk up the five red-brick steps into the main part of the garden, which is surrounded by a wooden pergola bearing a profusion of climbing roses.

Suddenly, as she is halfway up the steps, over her head but way out of her reach, a large Cabbage White butterfly flutters past her, and from a standing start, using the muscles in her hind legs, Otto springs many feet high into the air in a reared-up 'standing' position and briefly catches it between her front paws. Elvira Madigan take a bow. On this occasion the butterfly escapes to fly off safely, high into the sky. It is a remarkable display of the speed of her reactions.

Within seconds of her losing her butterfly we watch, impressed, as she springs up the pergola as if it were a main thoroughfare, and we see her disappear into the thorn-covered tunnel of the rose bower atop the highest arches. I gaze after her nervously and Michael gently mocks me: 'You will learn. You have to let them go. She will be all right.' And indeed, on that day, she is.

The very next day, however, she is climbing again amid all the roses when the calm of the afternoon is pierced by high, squeaky distress calls. We both rush out and quickly discover that the source of the sound is Otto, who is apparently jammed on a crossbar of the pergola over on the far side of the garden. Michael manages to ease her down from among the roses and we both inspect her, closely. Sticking out of the top of her eye, just above her eyelid, is an exceptionally long, menacing-looking thorn. I rush inside for tweezers and manage to extract it in one piece.

She whimpers dramatically as it is pulled out but then, forgivingly, licks my hand with her delicate, sandpapery tongue. We gently put her down on the lawn and she bounds across it in great leaps, for the pure joy of being young and female, and having the whole huge world in front of her to explore – and finding that it just gets better and better.

As we are watching her we are joined by Septi, lately emerged from the cottage, who has a remarkably sergeant-majorish expression on his face. His whiskers are very bristly and standing out, and he looks slightly cross and a bit ruffled. He sits in the middle of the lawn and miaows in a disgruntled-sounding way. Otto, indifferent to his chiding, bounds across the lawn and up towards the fence near the main road. Septi now, most emphatically, miaows something at her – and only at her – in his funny strangled-sounding voice. Michael touches my arm.

'Hey – Mo – do you realise what he is up to? He is

protecting her. He is trying to warn her not to go there.'

'No – don't be daft. 'Course he isn't,' I retort insistently.

But again, as Otto continues to walk along the fence towards the road, Septi makes his miaowing noise, and then he turns towards us, away from the road, and runs back into the depths of the garden and the far corner, which is without roads on either side. She is now watching him and, as he moves across the garden, she slowly turns and follows him.

Septi knows about roads; Septi has already lost some of his nine lives on roads. He did what he did with full knowledge.'Oh Septi – you angel,' I whisper.

Michael puts his arm across my shoulders as we walk back into the house. 'Septi will be her guardian. It will be fine, you'll see.'

CHAPTER 6

Septi and Otto, day by day, seem to become closer. We are both relieved, and amused, by the definite spring in Septi's step – and even detect a sparkle in his eye.

The old boy, truth to tell, had been whiling away most of his days, before Otto came upon the scene, in unremitting slumber. He would eat; he would sleep, for hours and hours, changing his favourite chair with the seasons – this being dictated by the desirability for either cooling summer breezes or which chair was closest to a radiator in the months the central heating was on. Just occasionally he would take the minimum amount of exercise a cat needs to take to stay in full working order.

This would entail slowly rising, shaking each of his stiff old limbs in turn, and then, with enviable languor, drawing his body out to its fullest length, first pushing out his front legs long and low with his backside high in the air; and then leaning forward with his shoulders high he would stretch out his back legs in turn, giving each one a determined shake for good measure. And always, while he did this, he would open his mouth wide in that head-splitting yawn that is singular to cats of all sizes from tiger to tabby. Following this huge effort, he would then saunter out into the garden to do what a cat has to do and to see off the enemy should there be any around, but even in the height of summer it was pretty rare for him to stay out all night, and never in winter.

Slowly and graciously Septi had seemed to be slipping down into a peaceful and ever more dormant old age. And now Otto is here and everything is different, for ever.

Otto bounds down the stairs and rushes around the room, greets everyone exuberantly and demands to be let out. As she hurls herself around the place, Septi watches her incessantly. At least one of his eyes seems always to be upon her. If she goes out, he goes out. If she demands food, he demands food. When she sleeps, he sleeps near her. The beguiling of Septi is now thoroughly underway.

One sunny day the cottage seems very still. The menfolk are out and about pursuing their various hobbies and I have been involved in some downstairs activity. I come up the stairs very quietly, wondering where the two cats have hidden themselves, and walk into John's bedroom. There on the sofa, under the window, the most extraordinary sight greets me. Septi is lying on his side and, at right angles to him, purring quietly, is Otto, who is clearly 'milk treading' with slow deliberation. She has her mouth clamped to one of his nipples. He too is purring loudly. As I stand there he looks across at me and shifts his body slightly with what, it seems to me, is a trace of embarrassment or perhaps discomfort. He stands up and the moment has passed. I pick him up to examine him and, with a little consternation, discover that two of his nipples are significantly inflamed. This worries me.

A couple of hours later I look in the room again and find that they are both fast asleep, curled around each other, with what appears to be the greatest trust that two cats who are not litter mates could possibly achieve.

I'm hugely moved by Septi's compassion, although thrown by his maternal role-playing. But why not? Many male animals are outstandingly conscientious parents and, if this is what the lady wants, he was going to comply. Dear Septi.

I am also concerned that he is going to be very sore, but shortly after this I observe that he turns his back on Otto whenever she comes with kneading motions anywhere near him, just as a mother cat would when it's time to wean the kittens from her. They remain very close, and sleep near each other more often than not.

CHAPTER 7

July 1998

Otto has won yet another heart in our household. Damian has returned home from South Africa and, animal lover that he always was, he has succumbed, fully, to her considerable charms. He remains, of course, loyal to old Septi, but it's very clear that Otto has bewitched him.

Otto has, indeed, powerfully imprinted herself upon all of us and it is not easy any more to imagine life in the cottage without her. Tiny, graceful, elfin creature that she is, she is irrevocably intertwined in the way we live now.

One warm night, as I'm lying on my back, head buried deep in the pillows, on the very edge of sleep, Otto creeps across the top of the pillow and gently licks my eyelids. The sensations of that rough tongue and the tickling of her whiskers are both wonderful and unbearable; eventually she moves away and I fall asleep. I start to dream. I see things somehow differently, my sense of smell is profoundly increased and my hearing strangely acute, but as well as these things my overall awareness is heightened to a point of near pain. In my dream I cannot see myself but I know that I'm a cat. I wake up and my metamorphosis dissolves but the recollection of it is disturbing:

> She came to him in dreams – her ears
> Diddering like antennae, and her eyes
> Wide as dark flowers where the dew
> Holds and dissolves a purple hoard of shadow.[1]

---

[1] 'The Tame Hare' by Norman Nicholson, taken from 'The Rockface' in *Collected Poems* of Norman Nicholson, ed. Neil Curry (Faber & Faber, 1994).

Otto has developed many rituals, some lovable and some strange. Every morning, when I'm bathing, she 'miaows' to come in the bathroom for a morning cuddle. She waits outside the door and calls at the moment she considers to be the appropriate one to be let in. This more often than not means that I, her slave, have to get out of the bath, as she just shouts louder and louder if ignored. By now I will have compliantly wrapped myself in a bath sheet so that she may sit on my knee. I stroke her gently and she purrs. Her purr is very quiet. You can hardly hear it, but you can feel it vibrating within her like a small engine. Sometimes she snuggles up on to my shoulder and licks my hair.

She is fabulously generous in her loving and will spend minutes on end cheek-rubbing and nestling into her chosen person of the moment. She will perform all of these things with Michael, John and Damian too. One of the rituals of the bathroom that she taunts me with is to run around the edge of the bath, almost kidding me she is going to slip, but doesn't – quite. So often she seems to just miss falling in by a whisker, but that feline sense of balance is truly remarkable. She adores the running of the tap and often requests to be lifted up to the basin where she both watches and plays, obsessively, with the running water.

One thing that she does, which disconcerts me terribly, is to wee in the basin; not regularly, just occasionally, but certainly unnecessarily, as there is a litter tray downstairs always available. She still uses the litter tray even when she has been let out, which Michael finds infuriating, but I know that it's my fault because I continue to keep one going inside the cottage, and I presume a ready-made litter tray is easier to use than soil that needs digging up.

She regularly makes me laugh by pausing very dramatically and, as she slowly raises her head, opening her mouth wide into a big but controlled 'O', which she holds, as if transfixed, for several moments. This is a completely different gesture from the small 'o' that is used when cats are cross. I am amused as it's a carbon copy of the mock shock-horror expression that my father used to adopt when I told him some snippet of information that he needed to allow himself time to react to. This gesture when adopted by cats has a different genesis. My mentor in so much to do with animal behaviour, Desmond Morris, indicates that this grimace – in Otto's case that is, not my father's – is known technically as the *flehmen* response, and is in fact the cat exercising its sixth sense or, more technically, its vomero-nasal organ.[2] She is taste-smelling the delicious aromas that are borne on the air or are embedded in the carpet in our fragrant bathroom. I think I would rather not dwell on why it is so richly delicious for her.

A further endearing habit she has is to 'forget' that the very tip of her pointy pink tongue is still sticking out of her mouth, and she will hold this slightly daft – but oddly appealing – expression for up to a couple of minutes before 'remembering' to withdraw her tongue.

One day as I'm lying in the bath, dreamily pondering these things, I'm struck by the slightly unnerving

---

[2] *Catwatching* by Desmond Morris (Cape, 1986).

thought that Otto's gestures mimic some quite specific habits that both my father and my mother had formed when they were alive. It would appear, merely from the dearth of evidence, that there are strict rules in force preventing the dead from communicating with the living, but if people who have died were to try to communicate, would it not be logical that they might adopt the channel of a favourite pet of the one with whom they sought contact as an obvious conduit?

I suddenly, quite badly, want to believe this. It would be so comforting and, as further fuel to the idea, it would surely be mistaken to 'block' an attempt by the beloved dead at communication. On the other hand, this way madness lies? I rise from the now shiver-inducingly cool bath and determine, once and for all, to rid myself of these nonsensical musings.

The month of July passes in a hot dreamy haze of sunlight, and one long golden day seems to slide into another, sustained by evenings of apparently endless twilight: the great solace of those who live in the northern hemisphere and know they must, in turn, suffer the rigour of short sharp winter days, leaving for work before sunrise and returning home long after sunset for weeks on end.

Otto, in this her first summer and with no possible anticipation of winter, explores every part of her expanding territory. She has now perfected her hunting skills in the butterfly department, the forensic proof of which we discover all too frequently in the confetti of broken wings on the steps leading up to the lawn.

Septi, still besotted, follows her around when she is on the ground, or even up into the pergola, but Otto frequently takes flight, too. She has a passion for heights – some cats do and some don't. If it is there and it can be climbed, climb it she does and, crucially, the higher the better. Our cottage has an exceptionally steeply pitched tiled roof and she has taken to walking along the very spine of this roof in an alarmingly vertiginous manner. She will also part-walk and part-slide down the steep sloping sides of the roof which are made up of tiny ancient (and irreplaceable) red tiles, some of which she regularly dislodges, so that at frequent intervals we have to rehang them. She frightens me so much when she does this, and if I'm around when she embarks upon her roof climbing, I cannot fail to be aware of it as it is usually heralded by the raucous calls of territorially jealous magpies.

Early one morning, just as I'm about to leave for work, I hear the all too familiar jeering of the magpies around the side of the cottage by the back gate. Having called Otto and Septi for some minutes and having failed to get a response from Otto, I trudge out into the garden and look up at the roof. There I see, high up on the tiles, the pathetically tiny outline of a small cat. As I screw up my eyes against the sun to see better, I can distinguish the dark red of Otto's mouth wide open and the sight is accompanied, above the hubbub of the magpies, by the plaintive mewling of a truly scared cat.

'Don't worry, Otto. I'm coming to get you,' I call reassuringly, to myself at least.

She cries out, yet more pitifully, and the magpies flap closer. They are big and they appear to be quite vicious.

She is young and inexperienced. I have no idea whether she would be able to hold her own against them and keep her position on that roof. I go off to look for a stepladder and realise that the only one that will get me high enough is the very long, hard to carry, painter's ladder in the greenhouse. With great difficulty I haul the ladder across the garden and manage to lodge it against the wall, but unfortunately in order to position it so I can reach Otto, I have to rest the foot of it on a high flowerbed with very soft soil and a lot of low-lying bushes. I'm wearing a straight skirt and tights, and as I start my ascent I ask myself if more than just a day in tatters lies before me. Otto continues to cry out but, as I ascend the ladder to its topmost rung and she first sees my head rising up above the edge of the guttering, she falls silent and edges backwards, higher up the roof. She moves over to the left and I stretch out my arm as far as it will go. The ends of my fingers are within a couple of hands' breadths of her.

At this point the magpies, who have been in full squawk hitherto, start to jump up and down in a semi-circle around her, making aggressive guttural noises, and I feel my mouth go dry as I realise I appear to be witnessing an ornithological haka. I shout out and flap my arms around to try to disturb them. This, of course, makes Otto back away even further, and as I stretch out to my fullest extent towards her, two things happen in quick succession. I twist round and find myself with a view that is completely new to me, over the end of the roof, over the high fence and gate, and down into the road, where I see a man walking by who waves merrily up at me and walks on. As I sadly register his misplaced jolliness, I feel the ladder, imperceptibly, start to lean to the left, as first it sinks deep into the soft soil on that side, and then from the sheer imbalance of weight continue its inexorably sinister journey. It happens in excruciatingly slow motion, and the sound of the clattering of tiles, the snagging of wisteria leaves, the cracking of rhododendron branches – as I, and my errant ladder, continue on our way – seems to last for five minutes.

When the descent is finally over and I am able to disentangle myself from the ladder and the bushes, I find, although bruised and slightly cut, I'm otherwise intact – albeit the owner of beribboned tights and a skirt split from stem to stern.

I start, a bit shakily, to ascend the ladder again and, once more, am fiercely resisted by Otto. 'For goodness' sake come down, Otto. This is stupid. Come on *now*.

At once!' I hear myself shouting, crossly.

But for the complication of being up a ladder, my feet would definitely be stamping in crossness. 'Oh Otto, please come. Please? Sweetie, come on! Please, please, please.'

No movement. She sits, hunched, staring, and then looks away. I hate her. 'Michael, where are you when I need you?' I mutter unreasonably.

I begin to feel sorry for myself and to care a great deal less for Otto. I climb down the ladder, having checked to see if the jolly gentleman of the street is anywhere in sight so that I might ask him if he could assist me, but the road is empty of all pedestrians. While I was diverting myself by falling in slow motion, a phrase (other than the standard expletives) had been eluding me, but now, as I scan the deserted street, I recall the words with taunting clarity: 'I was much further out than you thought. And not waving but drowning.'[3]

I go inside and make a strong cup of coffee. I can still

---

[3] 'Not Waving But Drowning' by Stevie Smith, taken from *The Collected Poems of Stevie Smith* (Penguin, 1985).

hear the magpies. By this time I am hopelessly late for work and aware that my excuse for not making an appearance is fairly feeble. I go out, torn clothes flapping about me, and climb up the ladder for one last rescue attempt. She is now right up on the ridge of the roof, by the chimney stack, and the magpies are about a yard away from her. 'Otto. This is your last go. Come on.'

She looks down at me with her owl's amber eyes. She miaows quietly and starts to come towards me; she edges towards the guttering and within reach of my hand. I grab her by the scruff of the neck and carry her down the ladder in one hand. Her body hangs kitten-limply and I transport her into the cottage where I manage, just, to resist shaking her.

As soon as we are both inside and the door is shut, she goes across to her food bowl and eats as if she has been without food for days. I make a guess that her voracious appetite is in reality a trauma displacement activity and, thus encouraged, I decide to enact my own displacement – or at any rate replacement – activity, and retire upstairs to get into fresh clothes.

And so to work.

CHAPTER 8

August 1998

From:	Marilyn
To:	Everyone
Subject:	BROADCAST: Kittens
Date:	27 July 1998 14:02

Susan Hill has a cat, Tallulah, who has just this week given birth to seven kittens, five of which Susan needs to find a home or homes for. I am doing this email on Susan's behalf, as Michael and I have adopted one from an earlier litter, by the same parents, who is completely adorable, and very brave with a most emphatic character – and if I was allowed, I would have all five!

They need to be found homes by mid-September – they are mixed gender and mixed colour, some tabby, some ginger, some tortoiseshell.

Can you initially email me back if you are interested? Thank you.

Marilyn

From:	Beth
To:	Marilyn
Subject:	BROADCAST: Kittens
Date:	27 July 1998 16:22

I'd be interested in a ginger one – keep me posted.

Beth

From:	Kevin
To:	Marilyn
Cc:	Michael
Subject:	RE: Kittens
Date:	27 July 1998 17:40

I think Michael should let you have them all.

Kevin

```
Puss . . . off!
  Michael
```

Shortly after this I receive an email on work matters from Susan, in which she signs off, philosophically: 'Love from Susan and Seven Kittens like the man going to St Ives'.

~

On 14 August John and Kathy come to stay for a weekend. John, an old and very dear friend from my distant past, has had a rough passage of health and is frail and wheelchair bound, but he is fortunate in having a tender and compassionate carer in his young partner, Kathy, and together they make it work.

From the moment that they enter the cottage, they are captivated by Otto. John, especially, is taken with her looks and her geisha eyes, but Kathy is not immune to her charms either and I watch the germination of the idea of having a cat in their life together grow in Kathy's mind. We discover that Kathy misses her old cat, Biggles, terribly and she knows that a dog would be too much for John to handle. I had never thought of John as a cat man, but then before his family had acquired their dog, Maggie, he always swore, very much in the manner of Professor Higgins, that he would never let a dog in his life, but he ended up being completely besotted by her, so I do know all things are possible.

As the weekend gently advances, punctuated by meals washed down with lots of wine, the conversation turns around on itself and, it slowly evolves, we are talking about Kathy and John taking on one of Tallulah's kittens. From this moment the die is cast.

Since late July and well into August there has been a steady drought and the atmosphere has become stifling and intense. For some days now the sound of distant thunder, rumbling away in the background, has created a sense of impending menace but the storm has failed to come to fruition.

During the heat of these several weeks, Septi has wandered around the place in a listless manner, seeking his favourite shady places. Mainly he has flopped out under the garden bench and the big picnic table. In the last few days, as the storm has come closer, his concern is increasingly perceptible; his head comes up at every distant rumble of thunder and his whiskers shoot forward in concentration. Now the air is electric with tension; it feels muggy and heavy. Today there has been an eerie grey light from early dawn, as the cloudbanks have built up to completely hide the distant sun. The sky is seething and rumbling, and contains within it all the plum, brown and black shades of dark bruising. The erstwhile dark edges of the great rain clouds are now engorged and have come together overhead to form an unrelenting black covering.

I rush outside to bring in the washing as the first thunder peals out and the great rain is released. At that first roar I'm aware of Septi racing past my legs and into the cottage. As I tear the clothes off the washing line I become drenched through to the skin within seconds. The rain is so solid that the strands of water appear to be motionless diagonals stretched out like harp strings. The force of the rain really hurts as it strikes my head, arms and back. The heat remains tremendous in spite of the downpour, and inside the cottage it's like standing in a warm oven. There is another massive clap of thunder followed, this time only seconds later, by a shaft of lightning so brilliant that everything within the cottage is illuminated starkly white.

I rush from room to room trying to find Septi, and keep shouting out for him, but he has completely vanished. I now call Otto. I'm unsure how she reacts to storms, and consider that this may well be her first truly spectacular one. I have not seen her for most of the morning. Because the rain is so violent I have shut the door, but can now discern through the hissing of the rain a plaintive miaowing from the other side. I open it and a small, protesting, drowned rat of a cat bursts into the kitchen, shaking herself for all the world as if she were a large retriever. Otto is saturated, but does not seem especially frightened or alarmed, merely outraged by the utter wetness of the rain.

I go back upstairs to find Septi and eventually track him down under John's bed. He is cowering with his head pointing away from the window, facing the wall. He is shaking with fear.

'Oh Septi, what dreadful trauma in your youth has caused this awful horror?' I enquire solicitously, but pointlessly. I try to stroke him but he is at that middle distance under a large bed where he is unreachable. I do not want to upset him further by poking him out with some pole, so for the moment I leave him be.

As I go downstairs there is another loud crash of thunder, and the lightning, with an extraordinary intensity, momentarily etches everything into strange monochromatic colours and then dies away. The rain is torrential and splatteringly noisy.

Otto, having managed to lick herself dry, in that paradoxical manner of cats, shakes each of her back legs in turn and saunters upstairs, apparently unaffected by all or any of it.

I look through the windows in the hope that the

impenetrable black might have shifted but it remains, ominously, directly above us. I'm standing at the sink when a seemingly endless roll of thunder, accompanied by simultaneous and jagged lightning, coincides with the electricity cutting out.

Finally, the time has come when I must comfort that poor old Septi, I reckon, so slowly I walk upstairs. As I do so I find myself wondering whether our old cottage has lightning conductors and asking myself why I had never thought of this before.

I walk into John's room and see that Otto has somehow, remarkably, cajoled Septi out of his hiding place under the bed and has got him to lie on the sofa next to her where, in true maternal fashion, she is washing him, meticulously, from head to foot. Although he is not quite purring, he is

definitely not trembling, as he was when last I laid eyes on him.

As I turn and quietly tiptoe from the room, I know that I leave the old cat in far better care than ever I could vouchsafe.

CHAPTER 9

September 1998

As time goes by, Otto becomes increasingly adventurous and little by little she expands her territory. Because I fear that she might get lost in her wanderings, she now sports a green velvet collar, complete with safety-elastic, with a disc on which is engraved her name and our telephone number. The collar also has a little bell which we hope will discourage her from hunting birds. She continues to climb the roofs of both our cottage and our neighbours' adjoining cottage – to our consternation, and probably the equal dismay of our neighbours,

whose tiles are under threat from her vigorous callisthenics. Michael and I go into the garden and look up at the high-pitched spine and see her etched against the skyline as a tiny black silhouette. We are mesmerised by her audacity, but we do also fear for her safety. In the end we leave her be, consoling ourselves with the ineffable truism that 'cats will be cats'.

She has, however, acquired another ill-behaved habit. When she climbs on to the roof of our neighbours' house, she will sit up on the tiles and, by her sheer presence, tease their big black labrador, Dante. We often hear him barking up at her in frustration and know that she is on his roof, taunting him with the feline equivalent of that human juvenile insult which consists of thumbs in ears and waving fingers while sticking the tongue out. What primeval instinct has made dogs and cats such enemies of each other? I know well that dogs and cats can be the best of friends if they are introduced to each other from birth, but their natural reaction, if not raised in a mixed feline/canine environment, seems invariably a hostile one.

My sister Margot and her family come out to spend a day with us around this time and she brings with them her much-loved Westie terrier, Snowy. Two things of note happen almost immediately. As Snowy walks into the cottage, Septi, who being an old and wise warrior would normally have ignored her, is forced into a reaction by Snowy, who bounces up to him and, in a manner that can only be described as confrontational, barks repeatedly in his face. Septi stares back at Snowy, holding his ground, and Snowy then rushes forward and threatens to bite him.

We will never know whether this is intended to be just a feint or not, as, without further ado, Septi calmly, but with dangerous speed, lashes out with claws fully extended and slashes open Snowy's black nose-leather. Snowy then squeals repeatedly in shock and pain, and

I'm much relieved when Margot assures me that the damage is comparatively superficial. Septi has trouble sheathing his claws again as they seem to have locked in a spasm, and as he sits back he looks down at his right paw, which he is holding out in front of his nose in a gesture that is almost triumphant, claws fully out, with a curiously philosophical expression on his face. We put Snowy out in the garden and shut the door.

Otto comes into the room at this point, having missed

the earlier fireworks, and, springing on to her cat platform, sees and hears Snowy outside the French windows. She is outraged and spits and snarls. We keep Snowy in the garden, but in spite of this Otto continues to glare at her through the window, with her back in full arch and fur erect, making the most hideous protestations in the form of growls and hissings. In the end we have to accept that the situation is irreconcilable and we shut the cats upstairs out of reach of Snowy and vice versa. Otto does not show any sign of becoming a dog lover, it would seem.

One Saturday morning I'm lying in bed, half awake, with my head turned towards the little square window. Lazily I am trying to determine what sort of a day it's going to be before I climb out of bed, when I see what appears to be a flying cat, bearing a passing resemblance to Otto, who, in mid-flight, 'hovers' on the tiny window-sill, scratches at the window pane and then continues on her earthward journey. It had been a fairly celebratory Friday night and a certain amount of red wine had been consumed, so momentarily I decide I'm hallucinating, except, as I wearily lie back, I recall that as the apparition passed the window it had been accompanied by the unmistakable tinkling of the little bell on Otto's collar.

Hastily grabbing some clothes, I tentatively go downstairs, wondering what awful sight will greet me, and slowly open the back door. Not a sign of any animal. I walk up the garden steps and round the corner and there, on the lawn, is Otto. She is sitting, rear leg pointing skywards, intent on an enthusiastic grooming session. I call her and, nonchalantly, she rises and walks across to me, completely intact. As I walk back to the cottage meditatively, I hear myself humming 'Immortal, Invisible, God Only Wise'.

As well as climbing things, and disappearing and generally being very distracting, Otto is hugely lovable. She adores to be nursed in your arms, on her back, like a baby, and a particularly affectionate habit she has is to wrap the pads of her front paw round your finger and hold it, gently, but emphatically. Many cat lovers have encountered the same gesture in their own cats and it is always curiously affecting.

Septi and Otto continue to strengthen their bond of friendship in vigorous play with each other, and an activity that enchants us greatly is their game of tag in the garden. Septi chases Otto and then Otto chases Septi. The rules are hard to work out but are clearly quite specific. Sometimes it involves Otto rushing up the pergola and sometimes, Septi. Rhododendron and laurel bushes are especially good for this wheeze, and it appears to be very important to keep hidden for very long spells of time before revealing where you are, and then when you do come out, you always have your mouth wide open in silent cat laughter.

Septi plights his troth to Otto in more ways than we will ever know. One day, however, his courtly behaviour towards her is almost more than we can bear. He appears to have concluded that if she cannot hunt birds for herself, as her hunting has been hitherto restricted, by size of conquest, to beetles, wasps, butterflies and frogs, then he had better do it for her. So, this old cat, having not hunted in many a long month, even in years, returns to the cottage one morning, proudly bearing in his mouth a three-quarters-grown blackbird, freshly killed, which he deposits before her. She, little madam, disdains his kind offer and hightails it off in the opposite direction, leaving the mess of body and feathers for us to clear up. I fervently hope that this is not a new pattern of behaviour developing within the old boy, and, for the most part, it would seem it is not.

And then, suddenly, the serious business of kitten collection is upon us. I have been busily trying to find homes for some of the seven kittens that Tallulah had given birth to on 18 July, and who are now ready to go to their new homes.

One, a tortoiseshell girl, is to go to John and Kathy. Two ginger boys are to go to Beth in our office. Two more, a girl and a boy, are to go to someone with whom Susan has been in touch, and who I have offered to meet on the A40 to do the handover.

I buy three luridly coloured cat carriers, they being the only ones available locally, and Michael and I stuff them in the back of the car and drive up to the Cotswolds to collect the five kittens. We get there to find that the other two kittens have, happily, already been homed locally. Susan is away but Stanley, her husband, helps us round up the remaining five kittens, and we finally get them into the carriers, two and two and one.

This time it's not good. As we turn round and head out of the drive, the kittens, probably each one inspiring the other, cry out persistently. By the time we have reached the main road and driven out of the village, the smell rather more than the sound of upset kittens is overwhelming and Michael and I begin to falter. We stop the car and remove the sodden newspapers in the bottom of the cat carriers and start again. The trauma, for them and for us, is then repeated, and again we stop to clean up. After we have been travelling for about half an hour, with the windows half open and trying to talk to each other loudly to blank out the heartbreaking sounds behind us, we realise that for five minutes now there has been a complete silence.

We look at each other.

'You thinking what I'm thinking?' Michael asks.

'They must be alive. They could not all just die like that!' I protest. I climb over the back of the seat and, by turning the cat carriers this way and that, am able to account for five kittens, all variously curled up and asleep in rather damp-looking little balls.

'Keep driving and please don't spare the horses. It's going to be rotten doing the handover because they look so ghastly, and they were so pretty and fluffy when we picked them up,' I wail.

As we near the outskirts of London, and employ the stop/start motion that is necessitated by the sheer volume of traffic on the A40, known locally as 'Leadville' due to the outpourings from the exhausts of the commuters grinding their way in and out of the city from and to Oxford and the north-west, the kittens wake up and become upset, anew. Finally, we see the BP garage, which is our first point of handover, and pull in and wait for the two girls who are to meet us to take the first pair of kittens. They arrive, late, having been held up on the equally tiresome North Circular Road. Gratefully, but also shamefacedly due to their condition, we hand the kittens over.

The girls peer into the bright mauve cat carrier and see a tortie and a ginger kitten cowering together, peering back at them. The kittens are bedraggled, and although we have tried really hard to clean them up, they still, all too clearly, reek of the expelled contents of their stomachs. One of the girls asks me, in a worried voice, if I'm sure that we are not handing over sickly kittens, and I try to explain that travel sickness is altogether different from any other illness and, that once they are home and cleaned up, they will be fine. I show her the other kittens, looking equally unkempt, but I have a suspicion that she thinks I have palmed her off with the 'B' team. They put the kittens into the back of their car and drive away, and I say a small prayer for both the girls and the kittens.

'Two down, three to go,' I say cheerfully. And Michael mumbles something that sounds suspiciously like 'Never again'.

We arrive at John's and Kathy's house in West London, where Beth has kindly agreed to meet us, so that we can hand over all three kittens in one go. After joyous introductions and a glass of much needed wine, we feel the time has come to liberate the kittens from their malodorous prisons.

Beth's kittens are two ginger boys, with adorable, erect, ringed tails, whom she has named Malachy and

Oisin. She is charmed by them and graciously forgives the condition that she finds them in. The kittens busily start to investigate every corner of the large room they now find themselves in, and we sit back and relax.

We have also released John's and Kathy's dramatically coloured tortoiseshell kitten, Delilah. Delilah – with her rich ginger, black and brown body and snow-white legs and white chest, and a glorious multi-coloured head, half black and half ginger, and the cutest pink nose with ginger 'pollen' splodge marks on either side of it. Delilah was probably her mother's favourite, as she is definitely the best nourished of the kittens that we have seen. She, of the three of them, most vehemently asserts herself and struts off towards the saucers that contain milk and food, travel sickness notwithstanding. She seems to know that this is now her home, but surely that is too whimsical? How could she?

At some point we all lose sight of one of the ginger boy kittens; he just disappears. There is an almighty scramble as those of us who are agile enough get down on our hands and knees to look for the young fugitive. Kathy races up the many flights of stairs in this tall house, searching for him, but he cannot be found anywhere. Eventually he is discovered, curled up asleep and looking wonderfully peaceful, on a low-slung bookshelf, atop a pile of venerable military history titles, no doubt grateful for the sheer immobility of his new bed. Beth, and her accompanying friend, are gratefully reunited with her pair of kittens. Meanwhile, John and Kathy coo blissfully over the audacious Delilah.

I adore this moment as I watch this little group of human beings falling, by degrees, in love with their respective pets. This minute is worth all of the cries and the smells (and the guilt) of the previous hours, three times over.

CHAPTER 10

Michael and I had booked our annual holiday for mid-September and it is now imminent. We have been going, for some years, to a house in a village nestling in the foothills of the Garrigues, hidden deep in the Vallée de l'Herault in the heart of Languedoc, where we return year after year and which feels to us like our 'home in France', but in fact it's owned by friends of ours who kindly rent it out to us.

We decide that it's not fair to ask John to look after Otto for the full fortnight that we will be away, as she is wild and hard to keep under control. Septi, on the other hand, is streetwise and could manage the odd twenty-four hours left to fend for himself. Also, he is uninjected, so no cattery will take him anyway, and the vet has advised us against injecting him at his great age.

The morning approaches that we must take Otto to the cattery and I dread it more than I had dreamt possible. Suddenly the longed-for escape down to our beloved retreat in the South of France is flawed.

Michael and I take her to the cattery together and I behave absurdly badly. I complain that the perfectly adequate cages are far too small, and when I hear the distressed cries of some of the other cats I get completely angst-ridden. I leave her special tins of food and try to explain to the staff why they have to be rotated etc., and am convinced that this won't happen. I make the mistake of turning round and seeing her face pressed against the door and her mouth open miaowing; an image that haunts me, repeatedly, while we are away.

The holiday passes uneventfully enough, and Michael is happily distracted by the fact that the last of the grape harvest is coming in all around us, and this is the best time of year for the locals if the weather has been kind. This year it's an excellent grape harvest. I feel unable to admit to Michael how completely bereft I feel by the absence of our small fluff-ball. My sense of loss is made worse by the fact that a family of feral cats, scrawny mother and half-grown kittens (one of which is undoubtedly brain-damaged), continually call upon the garden of our house. Linda, our hostess, has firmly requested that there should be no feeding of the cats so that they might be discouraged from visiting, but clearly the occupants before us have been feeding them anyway, so they cry out plaintively for the first few days of our stay. It is a mighty test of a cat lover's resolve not to feed them, but with difficulty we resist the temptation.

Two weeks later we return home and rush to the cattery to collect Milady Ottoline. She eyes us without any sign of evident pleasure; she turns away from us and pretends she has never met us before in her life. Always on the slim side, we note that she is a little thinner. I try to find out from two of the attendants how she has fared while we have been away.

'Fine, fine. No problem at all,' a young member of staff responds cheerily enough, but with the thoughtless ease of someone chanting a mantra, which curiously fails to reassure me.

Life, however, appears to return to normal on our homecoming and Otto is soon seen waving her wild tail from the rooftops in her familiar and mad way. Septi, at the first return of us all, does seem to be slightly put out, so it might be that he had relished being Lord of the Domain again. It's several days before any of us sees the two cats obviously interacting, and nearly a week before I find them lying near each other. Who knows what interpretation Septi has given to Otto's involuntary absence?

Soon after we are back I hear from Susan Hill that poor Tallulah has suffered dreadfully this time from the uplifting of the bulk of her litter. She has had to call the vet, who thinks, probably, too many of the kittens were taken at one time and he has administered hormones to stop her flow of milk and to help her to come to terms with the loss of her progeny.

Any signs of shyness have now completely worn off! Susan said they had never tried kitten food – but the boys are eating it like pros. Their appetites are growing daily. I'm feeding them the Carnation Milk, which is still an obvious favourite. The litter tray is another, less appealing, favourite. They play in it and scatter the sand everywhere.

I had a trolley next to the litter tray that had tea towels on it – big mistake. I've come home each evening to find my tea towels covered in cat litter, lying limp, half-in, half-out, of the tray. They use the trolley as a climbing frame. Found Malachy asleep in the frying pan that I keep on one of the trolley shelves.

Got to find a new location for the trolley. How's Delilah?

Lots of funny stories to tell.

TTFN. Beth

In early October my friend Annie comes to stay the night. Annie had made a bid for a kitten on behalf of her brother when I had been soliciting requests from would-be cat owners for kittens from Tallulah's most recent litter. In the event, he and his partner had decided against it, but Annie has always adored cats, and especially kittens, and is ready to fall for the charms of Otto, which it pleasures me to witness she does, wholeheartedly.

We have a long glorious night of reminiscences about life, death and the universe, and finally go to our various beds happy, but somewhat the worse for wear. In the morning, in spite of my self-induced frailty, I find myself smiling when I hear Annie's soft, pretty laughter rippling all round the cottage as she plays with Otto in our bedroom. After a less than robust breakfast, Annie makes her way home – and that would have been that but for a curious footnote to her visit.

In 1996 Michael had given me an engraved gold crucifix at the end of the Easter Vigil Mass, when I was formally confirmed as a member of the Catholic Church, and which turned out to be the last church service my father ever attended as he died suddenly and unexpectedly less than a month later. The crucifix had gained all the more emotional significance for us both, as, on one particular occasion, it had brought comfort to Michael's father, as he lay dying only a few weeks following my own father's death.

I am therefore distraught, on the Monday following Annie's visit, to discover that the crucifix cannot be found anywhere, and for several days I have not known how to bring myself to mention it to Michael. His mother is a firm believer in praying to St Anthony, the Patron-Saint-Who-Finds-Things, so I pray to St Anthony big time. Finally, I pluck up the courage and tell Michael. He is, naturally, very upset, but we both fervently believe that it will turn up. A couple of weeks go by, and then one day Annie phones me and we talk about all sorts of things to do with work, and also personal matters, and arrange to meet. Eventually we are about to hang up when Annie says, in a slightly discomfited voice:

'Marilyn, was there any special reason why you wanted me to have that gold crucifix?'

'Annie - oh Annie. Are you serious?' I squawk.

'Well, I'm serious I have a gold crucifix,' she chuckles.

'That is just so wonderful. I cannot tell you how I have been in agony looking for it.' We laugh and talk for some minutes and, although she never says it to me, I suspect she too is glad that it has been an accident. What sort of clumsy proselyte must I, otherwise, have seemed to her?

As I come off the phone I wonder how the crucifix and chain could possibly have got in among Annie's possessions, and then I remember that Otto plays with it all the time when I have lain it down on my desk. She picks it up, with her claws extended to the minutest degree, very delicately, and then throws it around, and on this occasion I had left it on the desk in our bedroom, and in the course of Otto's play it obviously just landed in Annie's basket.

Otto, the scamp, but olé for St Anthony and Annie.

CHAPTER 11

November and December 1998

John and Kathy come for a long-planned weekend
and naturally we invite them to bring Delilah, Otto's
younger half-sister. In fact, if the father is the same one
who sired Ottoline, which Susan believes is the case,
the same parentage (albeit from Tallulah's next litter
along) should, technically, make them sisters, although
not litter sisters. Either way, sisters or not, the weekend
is not entirely the feline success that we are anticipating.

Septi – although initially assuming a shocked
expression on his face when yet again a cat carrier is

brought into his sitting room and into his peaceful old age, and out steps another young female cat – appears on reflection to be graciously resigned about the intrusion. Otto, on the other hand, behaves disgracefully. That is, of course, in human terms. I presume that for her, as an adolescent, full female cat, now aged seven months, to suddenly find herself confronted by, on her own territory, another entire female cat, albeit much younger, must seem a highly threatening situation. The noise levels of spitting, and especially hissing, are considerable. I believe that Delilah with Septi alone would have been all right, but when she is faced with the dynamic of Otto, back arched and piloerect (managing single-handedly to look and sound like *both* of the fighting cats in Goya's classic painting *Riña de Gatos*), it's all simply too much for her to take.

After initially turning tail and escaping upstairs, Delilah does return to hold her own, however, and hisses back as good as she gets, but she appears, not surprisingly, intimidated by the combination of strange surroundings and hostile hosts. Who would not be?

On this occasion Septi does not lend his support to Otto in her aggression, and by the end of the weekend a mainly peaceful stand-off has been accomplished by the three cats, with Septi able to discreetly communicate from time to time with Delilah, while Otto maintains her distance, but continues to stare unrelentingly at the visiting cat, who might be from Mars for all the kinship she displays. Otto, at least, now restricts her hissing to *close* encounters only with Delilah. The latter is clearly confused by the antagonism but welcomes Septi's tacit gestures of friendship.

It is wonderful, however, to see the way that Delilah is a constant delight in equal measure to both John and Kathy, and how plainly they dote upon their beloved companion. She is growing into a very beautiful, silky-haired, tortoiseshell cat, although slightly sturdier in build than the willowy Otto.

Christmas approaches and we have to decide quite soon now whether to allow Otto to have one litter of kittens, or whether to neuter her before she has her first oestrus, which is likely to be any time from January onwards. Susan Hill has recently told me that she is going to have Tallulah neutered, and this knowledge is creating within me a strong yearning to carry on this fantastic line of cats. Tallulah's line seems to produce especially pretty cats who are, by all accounts, very loving too, and there is also the literary lineage that must be considered in the tradition of 'Ottoline Morrell'. I would not want Otto to have more than one litter, but perhaps just one? Each time I have sought homes for kittens, there have been more people who want kittens than there are kittens to go round, and I'm confident that we would find willing and responsible volunteers, on top of which I would like to keep one, or perhaps even two, for myself.

All my life I have wanted to have animals around me who would be allowed to have their own offspring, and it has never before been possible. That desire is probably why I have the adolescent need to play at farming whenever it's possible. I have, too, a strong wish to see how kittens who have been socialised from birth, who have been born in the house that they grow up in, will develop.

Michael and I talk round the houses on this one.

'Have you thought what poor old Septi might feel?' he asks me, ever loyal to his elderly companion.

'It'll be all right. It was all right with Otto, and you were doubtful about that one.'

'Umm – yes. But kittens, plural, is different. And who is going to look after them during the day?'

'They don't need looking after in that way,' I plead. 'Otto will make a wonderful mother, you will see.'

'Hey, what has happened to the conditional tense then? Where has "would" gone to? This is beginning to sound like a *fait accompli*.' He rolls his eyes in a martyred sort of way.

'No, no. It must be a joint decision. And also we should consult the boys too.'

But finally I perceive that Michael, himself, is quite keen on the idea anyway. John and Damian are both, in their chic parlance, 'cool', too.

The green for GO glows on the horizon.

◆

Christmas arrives and it is crisp and frosty white but there is no snow. There is almost never snow on

Christmas Day now, certainly not in the south of England. But, notwithstanding, Michael and I adore Christmas. I love the family gathering in and coming to stay. Sleeping bags everywhere. Heaven. It is always difficult, when working full time, to be properly organised, and I have now given up making real Christmas puddings in advance, but I love the sending and receiving of the cards, the buying of the Christmas tree, and the ritual decorating to Christmas carols from King's College Cambridge played on our old vinyl-playing record player, which must never happen before Christmas Eve.

For some years now I have used just tiny white lights on the tree and only silver decorations, so that the effect is monochromatically simple, and this year I managed to find a large number of multi-faceted silver balls, which we have added to the other silver decorations. On Christmas Day, after the slumbering lads have folded away their sleeping bags and just as we are about to depart for church, we go into the sitting room, letting in the cats for the first time that morning, and Otto runs amok.

Her frenzy is not for the toy mice or the cat-balls we bought for her and Septi, or even the catnip stocking (although she did rather like that – nothing like a fix on Christmas Day), but because the sun is shining through the French windows, hitting the countless facets of the silver balls hanging from the tree. As a small breeze gently turns the balls in circles, a myriad shafts of sparkling light dance up and down and across the ceiling, along the thick oak beams, over the tops of the armchairs, the curtains, the walls and all around the floor. Otto is lost to the enchantment of choosing where to leap next. She dances everywhere; round and round like a little dervish, pushing her paws out quickly by turn, trying to catch the tiny sunbeams. Septi sits motionless on the arm of the sofa. His expression is disdainful but he watches Otto all the same, just as we all do.

'Happy Christmas, darling cats,' I murmur.

Two days later we have snow, and I'm childishly thrilled because it makes it almost a white Christmas. There is a covering of about three inches, enough to change the landscape outside beyond immediate recognition, and presumably also to alter the familiar scents.

Michael and I let the cats out, wanting to enjoy their reaction to the snow. Septi, of course, has seen it all before, and does not, on the whole, appear to enjoy it very much. He goes out through the back door only as far as the bottom steps, raises his head, sniffs the air, then turns round and comes back into the cottage. Otto, on the other hand, is apparently dumbstruck. She bears the expression of one who is outraged because SOMEONE took the garden away and changed it. Having rushed out, she stops dead and looks around her in surprise.

By this time, she can feel the cold of the snow on her feet. She lifts up her two front paws in turn and licks them frantically. She shakes all four feet repeatedly. She bends her head down and snuffles the snow and then sneezes protestingly. She makes a very small miaowing noise, which sounds like a muffled question. She comes back inside but within seconds wants to go out again. This time she runs around a little but, we assume, the pain of the cold snow takes its toll on her feet and she comes back inside to the warmth of the cottage and to embark upon a mega-grooming session and also, possibly, to mull it over with the older and wiser Septi. As the snow outside hardens in the cold air, we can just distinguish the sculpted imprint of Otto's delicate footmarks, which stop halfway across the lawn and retreat back towards the house.

The following day it has all gone. So that was snow?

CHAPTER 12

New Year 1999

January creeps up on us and brings with it its baggage of gales, rain and a series of iron-hard frosts, the latter of which kills off all of the wild Irish fuchsias that we had, over-optimistically, left out in the garden. We had hoped that they were rooted deeply enough to survive a winter outside, but it was not to be. We do not get much more snow, however, and what we do get is only a smattering.

I was always heartened when one or other Dalesman would say, regular as clockwork on or around 26

December, 'Aye, well – the days are drawing out now.' Trouble is that they also used to say, on or about 26 June every year, 'Aye, well – nights are pulling in now', which I always found deeply disheartening. I can never bear to consider that summer might be on the wane, but most especially in June when often, it seems, it has barely started. By late January the days are discernibly longer and, as all those brave bulbs start forcing their way above ground, we can smell as well as see the change in the air.

Spring is on the way. Otto too is changing. She is restless and keeps miaowing to be let out, and then wants to come in again, and out again. She has started to follow Septi around and a couple of times I have found her rubbing herself against him. He looks perplexed by her advances. She will approach him, and then rub her head against him in greeting and roll over on the floor to play with him; she then rolls around in an amazingly sensual way, and her invitation seems quite clear. He sits very upright, front feet nearly together, and looks sternly down at her. He can look so exquisitely disapproving that he makes me laugh.

Otto's coquetry towards Septi becomes more pronounced by the day. One evening, shortly after our arrival home from work, she demands, very insistently, to be let out. Septi chooses to stay in. It is dark, but the light from the kitchen window illuminates the near garden and we watch her as she holds her head up, in a way I have never seen before, and proceeds to make a long, wailing drawn-out miaow that is astonishingly loud. She stays out for some time that evening. Much later on we hear, suddenly, the most extraordinary sound coming from the furthest corner of the garden. It's only possible to describe it as an ascending wail that then slides down into a guttural, harsh, bawl. This call, far louder than any human utterance could be, reminds me, magnified many times, of the complex scale of sounds that an adolescent boy can make, accidentally, when his voice is breaking but he can still sing soprano. Even I, with no cat language at all, recognise that primeval sound. It's the heart-stopping cry of a young animal seeking a mate. It's wild and almost shocking in its volume and intensity.

Michael and I look at each other. 'I have heard it said

that there are so few complete tomcats around that queens have to travel miles to find a mate,' I volunteer.

'Don't you worry, Marilyn! Any tomcat within five miles will have heard that one. I promise you.'

Septi hears it. He raises his head and his nose quivers. He seems ill at ease.

I'm worried for my girl. We call her and finally she comes in and we shut up shop for the night.

The following evening as we enter the house, instead of the cats coming forward to greet us as they normally do, there is no sign of them, although I know that they were both inside when we left for work that morning. I walk through the sitting room doors, into the dining room and there, under the table, I see our dear, aged Septi astride Otto, making a valiant attempt to mate with her. It's clearly failing and Otto is looking back at him with what appears, at the very least, to be a questioning manner. If it is possible to interpret a feline expression in human terms, then: 'Was that it?' is the only question on Otto's face.

As Septi becomes aware of us, he shuffles down, and back away from Otto, and slinks out of the room, with the air of one embarrassed. My heart aches for them both. I wonder how many times he might have tried, or was his one go just at this very moment as we walked in? As with so much to do with animals, we will never know.

Otto, needless to say, now requests, vociferously and unrelentingly, to go outside. We open the door and she races away like a greyhound released from a trap; we watch her until she disappears into the darkness. A little later we, and most of our neighbours I imagine, hear her brazen calls for a tom. Intriguingly, although her normal territory extends much further than the boundaries of the garden, in her search for a mate she seems to want to be firmly on home ground, and so the furthest point from which she has so far signalled her needs has been at the far corner at the back, by the garden-tool shed.

Another evening passes, accompanied by spasmodic, and sometimes raucous, serenades from Otto. Eventually, when I feel we cannot inflict any more of this on our neighbours, we manage to persuade her to come in for the night.

Thursday 25 February

I wake up early and find it's still dark, and wet; a most unpromising sort of day. I open the door to let the cats out so that they might perform their toilet. In Septi's case this is necessary, as he will not use the cat-litter tray. In Otto's case, unnecessary, as she will not 'go' outside, which is the fail-safe way we always get her back at night.

As I open the door, Septi steps forward, and then stands rooted to the spot, as if electrified. I hear the low rumbling of the deepest and most aggressive growl I have ever heard him make. Still snarling, he slowly turns and sniffs each of the posts flanking the back door. His hair begins to stand on end and he looks up at me with large eyes. I feel that he wants me to help him but I do not know what to do. I return his look, but shrug my shoulders helplessly. He turns round and walks firmly back into the cottage; he passes Otto but appears to make no contact with her. She bounds out and up the steps towards the lawn, passing the doorposts without giving them a second glance. She halts abruptly and quickly returns to now sniff each of the posts in turn. She then starts to lick one of them over and over again, with her eyes almost closed. We have to go to work, so I grab her by her neck and pull her inside.

On our return that evening I open the back door, with slight apprehension, to let poor Septi out – and again he reacts aggressively and fearfully to the scent marks on the doorposts. Finally, and with unseemly haste, he performs his toilet in the gravel immediately outside the back door; a place as close as this to the house would not normally be his chosen spot, and he returns inside with alacrity. We have kept Otto in while this has been happening, but now we let her go. Michael and I return inside and watch through the window. As she careers across the lawn, she suddenly stops, dead. She is completely still. As we watch her line of vision we see, some distance in front of her, a large, fluffy, ginger cat. He, for surely one so large must be a tomcat, is sitting down quietly, facing her squarely.

'He has style, Michael, I'll give him that. But I had not wanted it to be a ginger tom.'

'He's lovely – he really is magnificent. Come on, look at him.'

'He's too big for her. She is only little and she will have kittens that will be too big. Oh, oh, oh,' I wail.

Michael groans, long-sufferingly, at my contrariness.

Otto by now is in full flirt-mode and is rolling on the ground in front of her chosen tom. He continues to watch her – admiringly? Slowly he gets closer to her, and then, almost as if they are aware that they are being watched, they both move off into the dark of the shadows and we can see them no more. It goes very quiet and still.

A couple of hours pass with no noticeable sounds from outside, then the peace is rent asunder by a sound that makes my hair stand on end. I had heard about the post-coital scream of female cats but I had not expected it to be so completely blood-chilling.

'My baby,' I cry in anguish.

'Was that really Otto?' Michael asks.

'I'm certain. It's a really bum way to be made to ovulate, isn't it? Spiky bits on the penis pulling out rake her and make the process of fertilisation begin. But they say it's like the pain that some women experience when giving birth. Nature makes you forget quickly so that you will do it again.'

On cue, half an hour later, we hear another scream. We move towards the kitchen window and see at close quarters the same magnificent ginger tom sitting, tall and haughtily, to one side of Otto, who is looking somewhat dishevelled and uncertain.

'Mo, he's smiling.'

'Oh, typical man. 'Course he isn't.'

'He is. Look!' Michael insists.

I stare closely. He *is* smiling. I have never seen a cat smiling before – perhaps he always smiles. He is wearing a red collar and a disc is clearly visible, which somehow reassures me. He has a home and someone who cares for him; no alley cat this one.

As we watch them, Otto gets up and shakes herself and comes towards the cottage and asks to be let in, so we open the door. She is covered in mud and her fur is every which-way. As I bend down to stroke her, I find that the fur all along her neck is soaking wet, so her tom has clearly held her in check, as they have to do for their own protection.

She goes over towards the fire and sits down, then starts an intense and seemingly unending grooming session, which involves licking her vulva repeatedly, almost obsessively. Septi comes into the room, observes her quietly for a few moments, and walks out.

The following morning Michael is up very early and he lets Otto out as soon as he is up. I hear him calling me down to the kitchen. 'Look at him. He is like the Lion King. So proud and tall.' I look out of the window and see Otto rolling languorously on the ground, and a few feet away is the tall majestic fluffy ginger tom of the night before, watching her, from a respectful and safe distance, still smiling. We open the door to call her in before we go to work and she shoots back into the cottage.

The next night she goes out again. We hear her calling. We watch. But we see nothing nor, other than her calls, do we hear anything. She is out until very late and only comes back after repeated pleadings from me.

The following night it is the same, and for roughly a week Septi becomes a self-enforced prisoner within the cottage, and makes only the briefest of forays into the outside world.

For all that, though, we never see her ginger tomcat again. He came at her bidding, did what cats do and has now left for ever.

CHAPTER 13

Spring 1999

March rolls out, wild, windy and wet. The sporadic sunshine floods across the garden in waves, and as the moving shafts of light touch the daffodils and narcissi, that English frontline of spring flowers, the bright yellows are transformed into pure gold. In our garden this brash little army is then quickly supplemented by the shadowy purple of the crocuses and anemones and, shortly afterwards, by the lovely delicate misty blue of forget-me-nots, the pinks and whites of the early clematises and the glorious dark blue of the last of the spring flowers, the bluebells. Spring is such a beautiful and burgeoning period and it is over so very soon. Too soon.

We watch Otto for some small sign of pregnancy but any change in her size is so slight that it is indiscernible. She is due, soon, for booster injections, so I decide to take her to the vet, so that he may ascertain if she is indeed pregnant and, if so, forgo the injections.

In late March I make a veterinary appointment and when I arrive at the surgery I'm assigned a young man who is clearly not at all at ease when handling cats, and I embark upon the consultation with some trepidation.

The outcome is that he hasn't got a clue whether she is pregnant or not, and has to consult another vet in the practice about the dangers or otherwise of injecting her. I assure them that I think she is pregnant, not least because she has not come into oestrus again since her noisy serenades in February, and so the older vet recommends holding off the boosters until she has given birth. The young man says if I really want to know if she is pregnant I would need to get her scanned, and he hardly thinks it's worth it with, he sniffs, her 'being just a moggy'. I leave the surgery, mumbling crossly to myself: 'Might just be a moggy to you, mate, but to me she's everything.'

On 10 April John, Kathy and Delilah come to stay. We have a very enjoyable weekend in human terms, but it's even less successful than the first occasion for the felines gathered together. Otto is very disturbed by Delilah, her younger half-sister, who is in fact now neutered and no threat to her in any way.

Otto is just beginning to show a slight swelling on either side of her belly and, conspicuously, she is finding it more difficult to balance and jump and walk on the tops of doors, so we reckon her pregnancy is pretty unambiguous. I have also noticed that her nipples seem more pronounced and pinker, which is a further indication that there are hormonal changes taking place. For most of the weekend she lies on the top of a chest in the dining room and hisses repeatedly at poor Delilah, who although irresistibly attracted by this termagant above her, is doing her no harm whatsoever. Septi lies next to Otto, somewhat protectively it would appear, but at least he forbears to hiss at the glamorous visitor.

I find myself constantly apologising for Otto's behaviour, but Kathy and John generously forgive her as they recognise that she has much to distract her.

After John and Kathy return home I start to monitor Otto's progress more carefully, and become increasingly fearful that she might do herself or her kittens harm, as she continues to leap about outside as madly as ever. I'm aware that professional cat breeders would never allow their pregnant queens unconditional access to the dangers that lie out of doors when carrying kittens. I talk to Michael about it but we conclude that once she becomes a mother she will be tied down well enough, and for now she should have her freedom. So free she remains but, as the kittens she is carrying develop, she curtails her own wanderings and stays close to the cottage and its environs, and – to our great relief – seems to lose her taste for roof walking and other mountaineering exploits. She also seems to distance herself from Septi. They certainly spend less and less time together.

I know that the pregnancy of a cat lies somewhere between sixty-one days and seventy days in length from conception, and that the average is sixty-five days, so I start the countdown. I discover that sixty-five days would make it 30 April, which is arrestingly significant for me as it's not only my own birthday, but also, much more significantly, the day of the death of my adored father. I'm a little disturbed by the coincidence of this.

As the days go by, Otto starts to visibly balloon out larger and larger, and although she is clearly ravenous, the kittens inside her make it difficult for her to eat more than a little at each meal, so we are, and have been for some time, free-feeding her. I am amazed at how much such a little cat can consume. Septi is very gentle with her and in fact keeps his distance as if he in some way understands that she needs her space. He constantly checks her rear end, which presumably tells him some hormonal story. Otto makes little mewling noises from time to time, which I imagine are the noises of discomfort, but perhaps she is communicating to the young within her. She has, for days now, been scratching away on bedding stored inside the linen cupboard, jumping up on to the top of the wardrobe and trying to get into every single cupboard in the house. The instinct for a nesting place is very powerful.

I make arrangements to take holiday for the week that the kittens are due so that I will be with Otto in her moment of need. The one hitch to these well-laid plans is that, as part of my job, twice a year I organise major presentations which are held outside London, to which I may take several of the key directors within my company. Persuading my colleagues to agree to a date that suits all parties is normally a logistical nightmare, and the date for one of the biggest presentations is currently hotly under debate.

As the week of the due date for the birth of the kittens approaches, the date for the presentation is changed yet again and I discover that the newly agreed dates are to be 27 and 28 April.

'I can't bear it,' I moan to Michael when I get home.

'Well, you should just tell them, and say why,' he retorts.

'Oh sure. It's going to look wonderful, isn't it, if everything comes to a grinding halt and we are unable to do the presentation, and our excuse is it's because I was having kittens!'

He laughs, but his face alters rapidly when I continue: 'So you are going to have to make contingency plans because it's too close to her due date for us to leave her on her own.' So Michael, who is saintly and indulges me sometimes, does make plans, but it's awkward for him too and the cottage is filled with constrained sighs. He also keeps repeating, somewhat manically: 'But what am I supposed to do if she does give birth when I'm on my own with her? Do I have to boil water? And what do I do with it once I have boiled it?'

I reassure him that water is for human diversionary purposes only and he is very unlikely to need it, but that anyway I will be there, by hook or by crook.

I have set up a huge cardboard box on its side which I have lined with newspapers covered with an old soft white sheet and have put it down in a corner at the foot of our bed. I choose this site as Otto most often seems to be looking in this room for a birthing place, perhaps because Septi comes in here least often and she seems a little wary of him now.

Tuesday 27 April

I wake up this day, with all the material prepared for our presentation, praying that I will get down and back before Otto gives birth, for now, somewhat belatedly, I am beginning to feel frightened that something will go wrong and that she will be harmed in some way. I am filled with the foreboding that things will happen in the next twenty-four hours. I load the car up with projector, screen, laptop and kits and come back inside one more time. I stroke her gently; her stomach is now heavily swollen and she seems very tired. She lifts up her head before I go and nuzzles me.

'Oh, little one. I wish I could explain what is happening to you. Does your instinct tell you or does it not? You will be fine, you are one big brave girl and I will be back to look after you.'

She blinks and turns away.

CHAPTER 14

It's 5.20 a.m. on 28 April when my mobile phone rings, and I wake immediately from a fitful slumber in a hotel room far away in the West Country.

'It's all happening this end, I tell you,' I hear Michael whispering.

'Why are you whispering? What is happening?' I shout.

'Well, she doesn't look very happy right now. And I think she has had a dead kitten.'

'Tell me what is going on, please, please.'

'Well, she had one at about 5 a.m. I was fast asleep and I just heard this really loud squeaking and then

Otto miaowing and running around. And I opened my eyes and there was a small black lump on the carpet and loads of gunge and the black lump was squeaking and it frightened Otto, so she ran away from it.'

'And now?' I ask, heart pounding. At which point my mobile signal fails. I bang the mobile against the bedside table, which doesn't seem to make it any better. I grab the hotel phone and dial 9, then our number, and discover thankfully that I do have a line and I hear the home phone ringing.

'She's had a second kitten but it doesn't seem to be moving,' Michael says as he picks up the phone.

'What does it look like?'

'I don't want to get too close in case it puts her off,' he replies. 'It seems to have a sac over its head,' he adds. 'And it's ginger.'

I frantically try to remember what the books say about removing the amniotic sac and towelling the kittens down and swinging them round, and how careful you must be because they are very slippery.

'Try to get it in front of her face,' I urge him. 'Just push it under her nose.'

'Oh, she is licking it. She's licking and licking.'

'That's good. That's really good. Is there any movement yet?'

'Hang on. I'll just put the phone down and have a proper look.'

He is away an age; I screw up my face to listen hard. All I can hear is Michael talking to Otto in the distance. Then suddenly, and penetratingly, there is a high-pitched squeaking. Loud and protesting, and strong-sounding. Michael returns to the phone: 'It's ginger and big and fluffy and she has got the sac off him. He is nudging towards her and he has found a nipple. He's sucking - the black one's sucking too. They're both fine!'

I gurgle happily, but then he says: 'Uh oh. She has got up and left them both and is squatting down. She's straining.'

Long pause. I just hold the phone and my breath, and pray. Then I hear: 'Hey, well done. She's had another one. Otto, good girl. Good girl.' And, I hear later, with this her third - and as it turns out, her last - kitten, she now performs like a seasoned mother. She removes the sac, then eats the placenta with seeming relish, and licks her new kitten into mewling life. This one is a tiny tabby and an almost perfect replica of Otto, but with white eyeliner and no white socks and bib.

'Michael, you are a star for being there and coping with it all. I promise I will come home at the speed of light – and as soon as I can,' I sigh happily.

When I get to the presentation, Paul and Sue, to whom we are presenting, are very understanding about my distraction. Somehow we get through it, but my head is full of miniature whiskers and tiny squawks.

I hear from Michael later, however, that in the early stages of parturition Otto is not entirely happy with what is happening to her. After she had given birth to the little black kitten right in the middle of the bedroom carpet, which is when Michael must have woken up, he – the kitten – sets up a loud squawking, intended presumably to incite his mother to take care of him.

But in Otto's case it so frightens her that she runs back and forth around him and then, when she sees Michael heading for the stairs to find a bucket and mop to clean up, she follows him downstairs as the preferred option.

'She kept staring up at my face and miaowing repeatedly. She seemed to want help. I had to say to her: "Come on, Otto. You have duties. Back to your kitten," and she did go back, almost immediately.'

Reunited with her small black offspring she now starts to lick him, very roughly, with which he comes to life. He's so tiny he can hardly move, but stimulated by his mother he somehow drags his body by his front legs round to her belly and, with astonishing speed, finds and claims a nipple. This tiny creature with eyes firmly sealed (therefore totally blind), ears halfway down his head (and at this stage, stone-deaf), but with a keen sense of smell (so acute that within twelve hours he and his siblings hiss at any of us humans, the moment we are within yards of their box), displays that his instinct is 100 per cent in working order and he noisily takes in his first meal.

Michael, finding the cat and her kittens at peace, has decided that he must leave the cottage and get on with some of his own work. He leaves a message on my mobile to let me know.

I arrive back an hour after Michael has left and open the front door quietly to see Septi lying curled up in his favourite chair, apparently oblivious to the momentous happenings on the floor above him. He opens one wary eye at me and shuts it again. I pat him on the head and tiptoe upstairs, and as I go through the door into our bedroom I notice an empty food bowl and a saucer of water straight ahead of me. I look to the right, where I left the cardboard box before I went away, and there in the shadows is the beautiful Otto curled up on her side with three, tiny, sleeping kittens next to her. She opens her eyes, stands up and comes towards me; she trills a greeting at me and then, unmistakably, invites me to meet them. She looks at me, comes up to me and cheek rubs me, miaows, and then walks back to the kittens, and then comes back to me again and so on.

'Otto, you are so right to be proud of yourself and of them. They are adorable,' I assure her. And they are too, in a blind, helpless, vulnerable way. I left Otto as a singleton on Tuesday and return on Wednesday to find she is head of a family. I quickly get her more food, which she devours instantly. She obviously does not want to leave her kittens to go downstairs, so I make a mental note to keep food up here at all times.

While she is eating, I move the kittens to one side and change the bedding. I gently reposition them on top of the clean white sheet. 'There you are, Otto, complete with hospital corners.'

I sit on the floor with her by the kitten box for over an hour, enchanted by the marvel in front of me. She lets them suckle contentedly and I notice that the black one is down near her tail end, the torbie in the middle and the red one up near her head. Finally, they fall asleep and she turns over in the box on to her back. She has on her face an expression of extreme content-ment, but also about her there is an air of exhaustion, which is hardly surprising. I sit by their side, quietly, for some time.

Other than moving them on to the clean bedding, I do not want to touch the kittens yet as I'm not sure what Otto will feel about it; however, when I do ultimately yield to the temptation, she is hugely generous with them. She watches carefully, but she is sweet and trusting. I swear she is feeling the pride of maternity as much as she is on guard for their safety. I pick up each one in turn, and as I do so each one opens its mouth wide and emits a strong hiss of protest, the only defence open to these tiny vulnerable creatures. Ignoring this, I look them over to find perfectly formed little pads and claws. I observe their tightly scrunched-up eyes and folded-over ears and lightly touch their impeccably stiff military whiskers. Otto has chewed off the umbilical cord from each one of her kittens to just under an inch of each of their bellies; this is as it should be and the little stalks will in due course drop off. I am in awe at the instinct that compels her to do exactly the right thing to protect her young kits.

When Michael returns from his truncated day he

tells me that he has made a video of the kittens and
their mother, which he started half an hour after their
birth when they were still damp with the foetal fluids,
and later when I have the chance I'm able to replay it
and see almost how it was. Dear Michael, who at some
point in the video proudly and with real excitement in
his voice tells Otto: 'Brave Otto, good Otto. What a
day you have had, and you are so good and clever. You
just wait until Marilyn is home. Oooh, I can't wait to
see her face when she sees what you have done.'

When I hear this bit of the video my eyes fill with
tears. Yes, indeed, Otto; indeed, Michael.

While all of this is happening, Julie back in the
office knows that I have a cat who is about to have, or
might already have had, kittens, and she emails me as
follows:

From:	Julie
To:	Marilyn
Subject:	Kittens
Date:	28 April 1999 17:38

Have you got homes for all your kittens? One of our cats was killed last week. It was very sad – he was only one – but wasn't marked (killed on the road), so must have been very quick – and is now buried in the garden.

Julie

From:	Marilyn
To:	Julie
Subject:	RE: Kittens
Date:	28 April 1999 20:38

Julie – how completely ghastly. You poor thing. Oh I wish . . . we have such a small litter, only three, and we have seven people who want kittens. I will talk to Susan immediately and see if she has any.

Marilyn

I email Susan about Julie's plight and am delighted to hear from her that although she has just taken Tallulah to be neutered, it is not before she – Tallulah – has triumphantly given birth to a final litter (small by her standards) of three tortie girls and a ginger tom. I feel a pang of sadness that the days of breeding by the great Tallulah are now over, as she has mothered so many completely wonderful kittens. 'Down to you and Otto now, to keep the line going,' Susan teases me.

She has already arranged homes for two of them, but one of the girls, who looks much like Delilah, and the ginger tom are still to be homed. As soon as I hear the news, I quickly pass it on to Julie.

From:	Julie
To:	Marilyn
Subject:	Kittens
Date:	29 April 1999 21:33

I will email her straight away – it is
a ginger tom I'm really looking for,
so this sounds ideal. Thank you very
much!
  Julie

In fact, later in May, Julie herself collects her tom kitten from Susan's house and transports him directly to her own house in Oxford. At the same time, she also collects his litter sister for Jasmin, who works in our office at this time, and brings her into the office the next day. She is drop-dead gorgeous and is christened Millie by Jasmin. This Millie is to walk across more than five miles of London in search of a full tom, and is finally adopted by another family who look after her and her brood of hard-sought kittens.

It is anecdotally reported that full toms are so rare on the streets of London that queens have a tough time finding a mate, and the drive to breed in the female cat is an especially strong one, which is why Millie is to take such extraordinary risks.

An electrician, who lives in North London, is doing some work on our wiring one day and, as he gently fondles Septi, he quietly observes: 'I have a grand old boy like this one. He gets up to all sorts and I never quite know what's what with him.'

'Is he a battle-torn old moggy like Septi here, then?'

'Well, not exactly. He is a Burmese outcross. Very

good-looking and would almost pass for the proper thing, but he is not the same as he used to be.' He looks down at the carpet, frowning slightly, and I nervously enquire what has happened.

'Well, it's not as bad as I originally thought, so perhaps what happened is all right really.' He throws me a wan smile.

'Go on!' I laugh, encouragingly.

'At the time I'm talking about, he is about three years old. Anyway, one day he just goes missing. Sometimes, before that, he would have gone walkabout for twenty-four hours, but he always came home. A couple of times he had been in a fight, you could tell, but he had a really strong homing instinct. Well anyway, on this occasion I'm talking about, he just never came back.'

'How awful. What did you do?'

'Well, I used to go out every night and call him, and put all his favourite food out and things like that, but in the end I just gave up.' He shakes his head, sadly. 'This must have gone on for a good month. And then, one morning, early, I hear his voice – well, I reckon it's him but I'm not quite sure. He is calling me and he has some voice, my boy, I'll tell you. So I belt downstairs and open the door and I can't believe my luck. There he is all fit and well, and looking up at me for all the world as if nothing has happened and it was only yesterday that he went off.'

'But that's wonderful. So why do you say he is not the same as he used to be?'

'Well, after we had said our hellos and all that, I'm just standing back and watching him walk off upstairs with his tail up, the way he does, and I notice that they're not there any more.'

Suddenly he looks embarrassed so, giggling slightly, I ask: 'You mean he's been castrated?'

'Exactly that,' he replies. 'But it's a bit of a turn-up, isn't it? I mean, your cat goes out for a walk and comes back a month later with a squeaky voice and a new mincing manner.'

We talk more, but we both conclude that probably on the night in question his cat had been making a load of noise, as courting toms do to see off the opposition, and someone decided to hand him in to the Cats Protection League, who had done what they need to do to keep the number of unwanted strays and feral cats down. He did, however, have a collar and disc round his neck when he went out, but when he returned he was without identity. It would have been good to hear that cat's version of events, or perhaps not on second thoughts.

CHAPTER 15

So Ottoline, beloved cat of the household of Moon Cottage, at exactly one year and twenty days of age, on this sixty-third day since her conjugation with the smiling ginger tom, having issue in the form of three kittens, black, ginger and tortoiseshell, proves herself to be a completely wonderful mother.

We watch entranced, and every moment that any of us is at home we pay homage to the new mother and her kittens. Otto is an exquisitely big-hearted mother as she has no concerns about us picking them up and cuddling them, although whenever they squeak or hiss, which they invariably do when they are handled, she will appear quickly, heralded by the tinkling of the bell on her collar, just to make sure they come to no harm, but she never agitates if they are being held in the arms of a loving admirer.

My birthday follows two days after the birth of the kittens and Michael and I celebrate with champagne in the garden. It is hot and sunny and the kittens are asleep upstairs, but Otto and Septi join us out on the lawn. Septi has not yet ventured upstairs, as far as we know, so we are not sure whether he is aware that this is now a household of five cats, rather than the two of less than a week ago, although the kittens squeak tellingly when being manhandled by us. As Otto passes him, he takes the inevitable quick sniff at her rear end, presumably to keep himself up to date on her condition. What it says to him it's hard to judge from his inscrutable expression, but the smell of the milk alone that she is generating must tell him a tale. As Otto passes by in front of him a minute later, she gives him a cursory, but amiable, lick on his nose. 'And that's your lot, old man. She has other things on her mind,' Michael teases him.

It is a gloriously hot day and we indulge ourselves in our little enforced holiday, made necessary by our new surrogate parentage. I glance across the garden at the now recumbent but, I notice in the bright sunlight, slightly moth-eaten Septi, who is lying stretched out on the paving flags, panting. 'John told me last night that he thinks now we have kittens they'll finish Septi off,' I confide.

At that point we hear a wonderful sequence of bird-calls, which, a little belatedly, provide me with food for thought, and I pull a face at Septi. 'Hey, listen. Now that we have five cats you may never hear that sound again. Celebrate while ye may.' In guilt at my ornitho-logical carelessness, I shrug my shoulders philoso-phically and wander upstairs to check on the kittens, where I find their dutiful mother taking care of them.

Otto has in fact developed a fine technique of mothering. She spends much of the time with the kittens either feeding them, or cleaning them, but she has also established that she must get away from them, and is quite controlled in the time she spends with them. She does, however, stay with them for most of each night, every night, in the box in our room, and it is rare that I hear the gentle tinkle of her bell move any further away than to the other side of our room, as she seeks out food or water.

As soon as we knew that Otto was pregnant we had told people in my office that kittens were on the way, and had had a total of seven separate requests for a kitten, but precedence had been granted to Eve – friend, neighbour and cat-nanny – who very early on had asked us if she could have one of the kittens for her daughter, Jenny, to which request we were delighted to yield.

Tonight they come round to look at the kittens and I hear Jenny's happy cries of pleasure as she picks up each of them in turn. Michael has made his own bid, however, which is to hang on to the ginger one, as he wants to own a cat who smiles, and he hopes that this little ball of ginger fluff might take after his father in this and other respects. I nervously inquire which of the other two Jenny might like to own, but she needs time to think about it, so I must bide my time awhile.

We now have to postpone a long-planned trip to Ireland over the May Bank Holiday as we need to be here for this new family.

On the eleventh day following their birth, the ginger kitten's eyes are properly open. They are that startling azure blue of cat babyhood. The tortie kitten's eyes are slightly open, and the black kitten's eyes are still firmly closed. The ears of all three are still positioned a little way down their heads but are just beginning to prick up, and their hearing is slowly increasing. They are all able to haul themselves around by their front legs, using their back legs as levers to push forward their bodies. We have built a barricade of books to keep them safely in their box (but which allows Otto to come and go at will) while we are all out at our jobs during the daytime, but in truth they are not ready yet to leave the confines of their nest. At this stage they are still firmly in the neonatal period where they are completely dependent upon Otto to care for them.

By the fourteenth day the other two have opened their eyes and all three of them are beginning to move out of the box. The transitional phase has now begun where they remain massively dependent upon their mother but are ready to start seeking other stimuli.

One evening around this time, Septi comes up to the bedroom and takes a long look at them. He seems soulful, and Otto watches him warily. One of the kittens, inspired by curiosity, starts to crawl towards him and Otto, with great alacrity but in complete silence, interposes her body between Septi and her young offspring. The moment passes and Septi moves quietly downstairs to his haven of peace. I suddenly feel this is not the first time he has inspected them, and as he walks away his body language does not convey unconditional pleasure.

Kitten adoration from the rest of us, however, is in full swing. Damian and John are both in residence, and I can always tell when they have been near the kittens as the top of each of the kitten's heads smells of one designer after-shave or another, which leads me to conclude that the big softies have been planting kisses on the kittens as they come and go. They do not, however, know that I know this. Oliver also visits us for a long weekend and is almost permanently stationed by the box. I am enchanted, though not surprised, that lads in, variously, their late teens and early to mid-twenties should be as knocked out as Michael and I are by the considerable charms of small, fluffy, endlessly curious and irresistibly pretty kittens.

The kittens, now at three weeks old, are beginning to move around with more and more energy and appear to be fearless in their efforts to investigate each other and things close by them, although they show no interest in straying outside the bedroom. They play together constantly when they are awake, and at times clearly hurt each other more than they intend, evidenced by their loud squawkings. This is an important phase in their socialisation with each other, and this is when each kitten will lash out or bite if it's hurt too much by one of its littermates, so setting the parameters of how far each one is allowed to go. Their eyesight is improving all the time, although their focus appears to be slightly soft when, for example, we hold up a pencil or a finger as their eyes wander 'drunkenly' from side to side. Their hearing is palpably more acute and strengthening, and their sense of smell remains as well defined as ever.

Michael and I and the boys play with the kittens whenever possible, almost dutifully, as we are aware that at this stage in their development being handled frequently by people is paramount. Kittens that have not been handled at this stage may not develop into friendly adult cats. 'The peak time for socialisation is between

---

[4] *Veterinary Notes for Cat Owners*, ed. Trevor Turner (Ebury, 1994), p. 63.

two and seven weeks of age, and although socialisation can continue beyond this time, it's never as effective.'[4]

I am on continual tenterhooks, however, as I'm still waiting to hear from Jenny as to which of the remaining kittens (Michael having chosen the ginger one) she wants. It is right that she should take her time but I do long to know. We reckon that the black one and the ginger ones are toms, and the tabby-tortie is her mother's daughter.

Near the end of May, Eve and Jenny tell us that they would like to take the black kitten and are unconcerned whether he is a tom or a queen. He is to be called Beetle, and they are happily certain in their choice.

Now we may undertake the all-important naming of our two, and endless discussions ensue. Because Susan Hill started the ball rolling with the lit-kit idea when naming Ottoline, we decide it would be only fitting that all the subsequent cats from Otto's line be named in some sort of literary tradition. Eventually we name the ginger kitten 'Titus' after Titus Groan, a favourite character of ours, and we name the torbie girl 'Fannie', in honour of Fannie Flagg, an author with a big soul who once helped me to recognise and believe in human kindness again when I was a bit down.

Although the names are initially my suggestions, the decision is reached by consensus. Actually, honesty compels me to say that John has reservations about calling out the name Fannie. I do not understand this – Fannie is such a pretty name. Young men are odd, but he accepts it as her fate with good grace.

So, in order of birth, we now formally welcome to the world Beetle, Titus and Fannie.

CHAPTER 16

For some time Septi has been out of sorts, on and off. As an old street-wise moggy, he has never used a cat-litter tray, but Otto, who was trained to use one when first she came to us, has never been 'weaned' off it. Recently, however, Septi has been 'caught short' in John's bedroom, where he sleeps every night, so we have introduced a cat-litter tray downstairs just for him, although John will not countenance it in his bedroom, unsurprisingly. The experiment has not been entirely successful, and because John is now shutting his bed-room door at night, Septi, in what seems to be some sort of defiance of both human and feline social rules, is spasmodically excreting, in both forms, outside John's door – which makes it especially exciting for John if he needs to make a sleepy barefooted foray to the bathroom in the night.

During the daytime, Septi rarely comes upstairs to visit the kittens or Otto, and instead spends most of his time on a blanket on the Ottoman downstairs next to the radiator, even though it is not giving out any heat at this time of year. I have been aware, too, that when he jumps on to the piano from the dining room table, he not infrequently misjudges it and falls off. Is this the dreaded old age now showing itself, I wonder? His eyes are showing signs of slight cataracts too. He is definitely eighteen years of age, and possibly nineteen, so it would not be surprising if these were the results of the passing years.

I do wonder, though, if he is not also upset by the loss of his friendship with Otto, who has been distracted much of the time by her kittens. Since their birth, we have seen Septi attempt to flirt gently with Otto, and we see him in the garden still playing chase with her of old; but although she will play with him a little, her concentration is severely curtailed and she will stop, halfway through the game, and suddenly retire inside.

As the kittens grow, though, Otto restricts the time she spends with them more and more noticeably, and begins to play again with Septi. Now, at five weeks old, the kittens are practised climbers and particularly like to climb legs of the human variety, although anything that touches the floor and goes straight up will do. Their claws are truly needle sharp, and they have not yet learnt the 'polite' sheathing that an adult cat adopts (if you are lucky) when climbing on bare human flesh, so all of us go to work each day covered in a network of long, thin, red scars, which are immediately recognisable to all those who have ever lived with cats as the handiwork of multiple kittens.

Their play with each other is increasingly vigorous, and the protesting squeaks ever louder and more frequent. They run round our bedroom at breakneck speed and it is dizzying merely to observe them.

One day Michael and I are watching them fool around and it's evident that Otto is also trying to play with them, but she is clearly in two minds. Michael comments: 'You know, I think she's jealous of the huge attention they are getting.'

'Yes, I think she is, but also she's still half a kitten herself. She has only just had her first birthday and she wants to play, but her instinct is telling her she has got to be responsible. Poor Otto. What a dilemma.'

In fact, she has been supremely responsible. She has fed and cleaned them impeccably. As is the way of all feline mothers, she has meticulously cleaned their faeces away, right up to the point when they started to eat a small amount of dried food. From that moment on, different rules came into play and she left them to figure out what the cat-litter tray is for. Fannie and Beetle have worked it out; Titus seems OK with the principle but a little backward in practice. Sometimes he makes it and sometimes he doesn't, but he is getting better at it. I am reminded of what many human parents say of their babies at the time of weaning: babies' nappies when the baby is milk-fed have a purity of smell that only changes the moment solids are introduced into the diet.

So already the kittens are losing their babyhood – so quickly. Otto comes to them now to feed them only perhaps three times a day, and no longer spends the night with them, although she will visit them nocturnally. In spite of this, they have never ventured out of this one room to find her. When she decides to feed them now, she comes to the open bedroom door and summons them with a special miaow that she uses just for them. Fannie, whom Michael calls 'mummy's little girl', always stops doing whatever she is about and immediately runs up to her increasingly imperious mother. Beetle and Titus may or may not stop what they are doing, depending on the mood they are in. Otto will lie down to be suckled, but for only a few minutes at a time. The kittens by now also have needle sharp teeth, which cannot be comfortable for their mother.

When they were two weeks and under, they used to swap with each other for their nipple of choice, but now they have their regular feeding positions. Beetle goes to the top end near Otto's head, Titus chooses the middle, and Fannie the tail end. In large litters, 'ownership' of a favoured nipple prevents ongoing battles between siblings. Beetle and Titus are much larger and also fluffier now than Fannie, with much larger feet, too. Of the three kittens, Fannie is the most active. She is, however, the most delicate and is very girly-looking; she is as close to a clone of her mother as it's possible to imagine from a natural birth. Beetle is pure black, from top to toe; there is not a whisper of white anywhere on him. He has black nose leather and black footpads, and just the merest hint of even blacker stripes through his shiny black fur. He is a magnificent-looking kitten. Titus is a light red marmalade cat, with white chest and tummy and socks, and remarkably long, stiff, white whiskers – much larger whiskers than the other two. Fannie and Beetle have tiny little 'o' mouths, like their mother, and Titus has the big smiley mouth of his father that Michael so yearned for. They all still have their baby-blue eyes, but these look as if they might be about to change. Their ears are now properly up on the top of their heads and strong and pointy and stiff.

In spite of these outward signs, I do not fully appreciate exactly how fast the kittens are developing until something happens that makes me think again.

It is early evening and the kittens are now just over six weeks old. I am sitting at my desk in our bedroom reading a book and have my back to the door when I hear Otto making her special 'calling all kittens' miaow. Without turning round, I presume that they will go to her and that she is about to feed them. I hear it again and the tone has changed, but I continue to ignore it, until I hear it a third time. I then realise, suddenly, that the sound is coming from outside the bedroom, which is not at all characteristic. I get down from my chair quietly and walk across the room, and slowly open the door on to the landing. In front of me is a remarkable tableau.

Lying facing me is Otto stretched out with her back against the door of the bedroom on the other side of the landing. Between her and me are the three kittens.

They are sitting bolt upright in a tiny semi-circle and all of them have their front feet placed neatly together. Each one of the kittens in turn is tipping its head from one side to the other, watching its mother in a concentrated kind of way. Otto is making the low 'chchchchch' noises of a cat who has seen a bird and, as I too watch, I'm horrified to see that she is batting, back and forth, between stretched-out forepaws, a tiny brown fieldmouse who, probably from pure fear, seems now close to catatonic paralysis. I glance down the stairs and see Septi looking up, watching every move with the impassive attentiveness of a long-serving umpire on Centre Court.

'Hey, this sure isn't the moment for a killing lesson. Not here, not now, not nohow,' I protest. I scoop the now almost motionless mouse, who is himself not much older than the kittens, judging by his size, into an empty tooth mug and take him across the road and gently tip him out on to an enclosed bit of wild land where Otto and Septi are unlikely to go. He doesn't move, so I fear he may already be dead from fright, although he is still warm.

When I come back and tell Michael about the lesson on the landing that I have just witnessed, he says: 'So that was what the commotion was about. I reckon that Septi hunted that mouse down for Otto as some sort of offering.'

'It's true that recently Otto and Septi seem to have bonded again and are spending much more time out and about together, so no doubt the old boy did think it would be helpful. Perhaps she put in a special request?' I wonder aloud.

Ironically, shortly after this event I received the following email:

From:	Beth
To:	Marilyn
Subject:	Birds
Date:	8 June 1999 11:40

Oisin and Malachy have killed! They

caught a blackbird this morning, brought it through the cat flap, then lost control of it, blackbird started to fly around my bedroom until it was trapped behind the curtain. In the meantime, I opened the front door, then threw a sweatshirt over Oisin. The bird flew out of the door. Malachy went after it and caught it again. I finally got them off the bird and put it in a box and took it away to die in peace. Ugh.

Of course, they both think they're hot stuff. I was left cleaning birdshit off my bedroom window and curtains.

Beth

The very next day, following the hunting lesson, Otto and Septi spend hours playing their complicated game of chase round the garden. Septi has always been a strong climber, but Otto can out-climb him with ease, so when the game is finally called to a halt it's usually because Otto has disappeared into the thorny tangle of the roses which have twisted their way up through the pergola, and Septi gives up the chase. This day, however, I see Otto veering off after Septi, through two sides of the tunnel formed by the roses on the pergola, round under the wall of the greenhouse, up over the compost heap, and down by the bike shed – where she called for her tom to come to her – back under the laurel bush and out into the open garden right in the middle of the lupin beds. A little while later I go out and see that Septi is now chasing Otto. He is still more skilful at hiding himself than she is, and as I watch he waits down below the steps, and then he sneaks across and crouches under the lavender bushes from which vantage point he jumps out, surprising her. They play for what seems like hours. Finally, they both flop down on to the cooling stone flags and lie with their mouths open in the silent laughing way they have together.

I am so glad that they have not lost that special companionship that they have established.

CHAPTER 17

Midsummer's Day – Monday 21 June 1999

Shortly before 8 p.m. the telephone rings. I answer it and a woman's voice says: 'Do you have a cat called Otto?'

There is a slight pause on her end of the telephone, and then I hear: 'Rather, I should say, *did* you have a cat called Otto?'

My world slides on its axis. I feel sick with fear. Shortly after she finishes her second sentence, I hear my own disembodied voice, shouting, pointlessly:

'No. No. No. No. No.'

I fight for control. 'What happened?' I ask.

'She was run over.'

'Where are you?' I finally manage.

'Outside your front door,' she replies.

I call for Michael out of the window, but he has heard my agitated voice and knows beyond doubt, in the way that a loved one always does know, that something terrible has happened. We open the door together and a young man is standing there with a black bin liner in his arms.

'I'll bring her in and you can bury her in the garden,' he says. He then adds: 'The lady who rang you has had to go home.'

We go out through the sitting room where Septi is asleep on the sofa and out into the back garden.

'I need to see her,' I whisper.

'She doesn't look very nice.'

Michael and I carefully unwrap her from her prosaic shroud. She is warm and soft and, as I put my nose to her fur, I'm overwhelmed by the singular sweet smell that is special to her. Her mouth and nose are bashed, but otherwise her body seems intact. She is deceptively pliable. I swear I can see her breathing.

I look up at Michael. He has tears in his eyes. 'Oh Otto. Poor Otto, why this?' he chokes.

'Are you sure she's dead?' I plead. 'She looks as if she might just be unconscious.'

'I promise you she is dead,' the young man replies.

I lay her gently on the ground and put my hands all over her, trying to find a heartbeat. It's completely impossible to accept that this life has just been snuffed out. As I'm touching her and watching, hope against hope, for some sign of life, I see a small trickle of milk leaking out from one of her nipples. Upstairs there are three kittens that are waiting for their mother. I pick her up in my arms and bury my face in her fur.

'Otto, you are the best cat in all the world. You are so brilliant and so lovely. How can we live without you? Any of us? Why, why, why, did you have to go and get yourself killed? Otto, come back.'

I gently stroke her poor flat lifeless body, willing life to come back into it, but in reality saying farewell. I fondle her pert ears, the way she likes it best. I stroke her soft shiny still warm fur and imagine that I hear the thrum of her little purr. I touch her four white socks in memory of the giddy dances that she danced, and finally I pick her up and snuggle her head down on my shoulder in the hope that she might lick my neck, like she does, just one last time. 'You never said goodbye.'

Michael disappears inside to find John and tell him what has happened. John comes out shortly afterwards because he wants to be the one to dig her grave. He starts to dig a hole under the rhododendron bush where she used to play hide and seek so often with Septi. As he digs, with the apparent determination of an escapee who knows he has only one bid for freedom and this is it, I see the tears running down off the end of his chin. He later claims this was sweat, but all the same my heart goes out to him for the pain he feels, as it does to Michael, who is being strong for all of us, but who is patently shattered by the loss of our little cat. As John covers her body with the final layer of soil over her hugely deep grave, Michael and I whisper a prayer to send her on her way.

The young man stays for a drink and we talk about Otto. He says: 'She was a remarkably beautiful cat.'

I cannot bear it. I cannot bear her being *was* and not *is*. I am suddenly overwhelmed with a sense of how very wicked I must have been to need to be punished in this manner and to this degree. This is a very egocentric thought, as others are hurt by Otto's death as well as me, but it haunts me.

We open another bottle. The young man tells me that the woman who phoned me is from the Cats Protection League, and that she had said to him that anyone living on our road and keeping cats needed their heads examining. So that is comforting, but she may well be right. The woman had rung him because he lives on one of the boats on the canal nearby and she had thought it was his cat. He came out with his heart in his mouth, but found that it was not his cat after all. I ask him exactly where it happened. He tells us that Otto's body was found five yards away from our front door on the other side of the road opposite our neighbours' house. Impossible to tell which way Otto was going, but she must have been hit just once at high speed and flung into the gutter by the force of the car.

'Cats are fantastically fragile, you know. It really does not take much to kill them, and if they are hit by a car, that is pretty much that,' he said.

The driver had driven on, but maybe without even knowing that a cat had been killed. The young man leaves shortly afterwards, but I am touched by his consideration and feel deeply sorry for him in having to cope with us at this time.

Michael's brother, John, half-Irish as Michael is, and a priest, has been staying with us for the weekend. Today he has been out visiting friends and arrives back amid this scene of deep mourning. As soon as he walks through the door, we take him round the garden and tell him every detail of what has happened for the umpteenth time, and Michael points out where the dogs of the previous owner are buried, under the apple tree, and then where we have just buried Otto across the other side of the lawn, and John murmurs: 'Ah, cats on one side, and prots, sorry, dogs, on the other.'

Bless him for the gift of giving us laughter.

CHAPTER 18

Later on in the evening we realise that Septi has gone missing and we go out in search of him. We look everywhere, and eventually we find him on the waste-land across the other side of the hateful main road that killed Otto.

'Michael, I'm sure he's looking for her.'

'Do you reckon? Don't you think he saw us burying her?'

'I think all that went over his head, and she was in a bin liner when she came into the house so he may possibly not have smelt her.' Finally, we persuade Septi to come back inside and we close up for the night.

Never has the 'longest day' seemed truer.

At regular intervals through the night the kittens in turn squeak out. I presume they are calling for Otto as they have never made this noise before, certainly not at repeated intervals. I hear them get up and go across to the food and water again and again. They have all been eating solids for a few weeks now and they are fortunate, as orphans go, that they have at least had their mother for the first seven and a half weeks of their life, and have even had one hunting lesson, so they are of an age where they can now live independently. A few weeks back and the story would have been very different. It is startlingly painful, however, to hear them suffer this first night of life without a mother.

In the morning Septi is restless, so Michael lets him out early. I rise shortly afterwards, and as I enter the bathroom I hear a noise that arouses my curiosity. I open the window and the sight that greets me breaks my heart anew.

Outside the bathroom window, in a little alley that leads out on to the main road, we have placed a very tall water butt, and sitting on top of this water butt is

Septi. He has his head turned away from the cottage and is staring straight down the road towards the distant traffic lights. He is making his strangulated 'miaow' over and over and over again. I feel certain, from observation, that miaowing is for him a huge effort, but at this moment it seems as if he will never give up. He is calling Otto. I'm sure of it.

So poor Septi. No one knows how to tell him that his beloved kitten, his playmate, his queen, the beguiling elfin creature who has filled his old age with sunlight and laughter, is never coming back, however hard he calls. I burst into tears and Michael comes running up and hugs me. I helplessly indicate what I can see. Michael looks out and nods compassionately. He goes straight down and out through the front door and picks Septi up in his arms and, talking gently to him the while, he carries him back inside.

While all of this has been going on another phase is also beginning. Miserably I'm trying to get us some breakfast, before leaving for work, when I hear a bump and a couple of scuffles. I walk into the dining room and see the tiny figure of Fannie appearing round the corner from the bottom of the stairs, followed by a plopping, falling sound, and then Titus appears. I stick my head up the stairs and, sure enough, two stairs higher up Beetle is suspended half on one stair and half on the other.

Although the flight of stairs in the cottage is short, only ten steps in all, because the cottage is very old, the steps are fiercesomely steep. Some time in the 1600s this cottage would have been a farm labourer's dwelling place and the upper floor would have been the hayloft. This is what has deterred the kittens from venturing further than the bedroom and the landing, but possibly they now think that their mother is playing another training game on them and, if they show enough enterprise, they will be rewarded by seeing her.

I groan. 'Now what do we do?'

Michael, with savvy, suggests: 'While we are out, can't you just keep them shut in our bedroom, and then when we are here we can just let them be?' And so that is how it is for the first day after Otto's death.

That night when we get back, we let Septi out and we open the bedroom door and see what the kittens will do. Septi returns to the water butt and calls for his ladylove. In all the time we have lived here, he has never sat on that water butt and miaowed until now. It's so hard hearing it, but Michael thinks we should just let him do it.

'He needs to be allowed to grieve just as we all do.'

'But he's calling for her?'

'Same sort of thing.'

Septi continues to call for Otto for nearly ten days, but eventually he becomes dispirited and gives it up. He now spends much of his time outside. The weather is hot, and also the kittens now have the run of the house.

The kittens, meantime, are displaying the astounding resilience of extreme youth, bordering on apparent insensitivity, even. They jump exuberantly over the furniture, they fight roly-poly tussles with each other, they throw cat litter around everywhere, they start climbing up the curtains, they discover the mantelpiece. A whole new world opens up to them. I am sure that they do miss Otto, but young fit animals have a hugely strong sense of survival and that is where their energies are being spent.

It is strange, however, that for days on end I can hear in the far distance the tinkling of the bell on the collar of that little cat. Somehow she is still coming to me in dreams . . . her eyes wide as dark flowers.

CHAPTER 19

Going into the office the next day is as all right as it could be and my boss, rather endearingly, manages to make me laugh by his reaction to my tale of the unforgettable tense change of the woman on the phone, as she switches her question so brutally from current ownership to past ownership of a cat called Otto. 'Ah! A member of the Sensitive School of Counselling!' he suggests.

Friends and colleagues are sympathetic, and I am aware that it's unreasonable of me to mind when one says: 'Anyway, you have the kittens to take her place.'

True, but Otto is irreplaceable. The death of a loved

one is an annihilation beyond just the existence of that being. Death kills something inside of oneself too. There is a marvellous observation by one of Anne Tyler's characters, Poppy, about his long-dead wife:

> 'People imagine that missing a loved one works kind of like missing cigarettes,' he said. 'The first day is really hard but the next day is less hard and so forth, easier and easier the longer you go on. But instead it's like missing water. Every day you notice the person's absence more.'[5]

However, because I know that animal bereavement is an embarrassment for anyone who has not experienced it, rightly or wrongly I have decided that I need to be 'grown up' about it and not talk about it to anyone.

My self-enforced regime of stiff upper lip might, just might, therefore be the reason why, when some days

---

[5] *Back When We Were Grown-ups* by Anne Tyler (Vintage, 2002).

later I am sitting at a long, linen-clad, inexpressibly elegant dining table in a garden of supreme beauty in the grounds of a manor house in the depths of Wiltshire, I find myself, suddenly, behaving badly or, at the least, questionably. It is a gloriously hot summer's day and the long table in question is set out under the especially welcome shade of a group of trees. An atmosphere of well-being and tranquillity is enhanced by the steady flow of gentle conversation and sporadic ripples of laughter among the fourteen or so guests around the table, aided by the copious refills of fine wines supplied by an immaculately clad *sommelier*. A luncheon party of sumptuous proportions is under way and, as part of my job, I have been included in the guest list.

Our very kind hostess is on fine form and I am fortunate to be seated near her. I'm much taken with her superb Irish wolfhound who is the finest I have ever seen, and who is called Gideon. He spends much of the lunch gently nudging those of us sitting at his end of the table with his warm, wet nose, and even though all his four feet are firmly on the ground, he nevertheless towers above us. Our hostess, confidingly, informs us that they have had a visit from a vet only the week before who had collected sperm from Gideon to be stored on their behalf.

'Twice within the hour,' she boasts, triggering a round of applause and cries of admiration (from those of us who are within earshot and to the lasting mystification of those further up the table) at Gideon's prowess. The purpose of this exercise is that because the magnificent Gideon is now of some age, she would hate something to happen to him and so, by default, for his line to cease to exist; therefore, with his sperm being held, there is just a chance, with the benefit of AI, that they would be able to have his puppy at some point in the future.

Probably because the day is so glorious, the food wonderful, the company stimulating and she herself is such a sympathetic person, I find myself, unforgivably, starting to talk about Otto and my eyes fill with tears. This sweet woman rushes round from her place at the head of the table to the side of my chair. She flings her arms around me comfortingly and cries:

'Oh Marilyn, please. You can take home some of Gideon's sperm.'

Laughingly, I turn down her kind offer, but am compelled to say: 'Never could anyone have tried to comfort another person in their loss with such gracious generosity and such truly lateral thinking. Thank you, thank you, and you too, Gideon.' He puts his head on one side but makes no remark.

That lunch is a truly cathartic one for me. The pain resulting from the bereavement of an animal who has been much loved can be every bit as sharp and sickening and long-lasting as human bereavement. It is not always so, but if compassion can be shown to those who are suffering it, who may, God forbid, want even to talk about it, it might help them tremendously.

I have made an appointment to attend my local veterinary clinic as the time has now come for the official sexing of the kittens and for them to have the first of their two lots of injections. I talk to the receptionist about what makes a good 'cat vet' as I discover that the young man who was unable to tell me whether Otto was pregnant or not has also written her up in his notes as 'dangerous' – and a less dangerous cat than Otto is hard to imagine. We are assigned Pat, who is indeed first class with the feline species.

First, though, I need to get the kittens there. A simple task, I think. I'm so wrong. I have recently acquired a large mesh cat cage, which means that the captive travellers can have a fine view of all that is around them, and which I hope may make them less panicky than the enclosed carriers that I had used to transport Otto and her various half-sisters and brothers. I duly place the three kittens into the cage and carry it out across the main road to put it in the car. From the very moment that I place the cage in the car, the most terrible caterwauling starts up. At first it is Fannie rendering an ear-shattering solo. I start the engine and ease the car out on to the road. Now Titus and Beetle join in lustily, but the sound is wholly lacking any harmony; it's an indescribably dreadful noise.

As I turn the car from the first roundabout down towards the second, I can see out of the corner of my eye a small tabby body squeeze its way straight through the mesh on the corner of the cage and jump down into the footwell where my feet are pumping the clutch and brake pedals. Terrified lest she get under the brake pedal and I crush her tiny body, I go round the roundabout twice before finally daring to brake enough to bring the car to a halt, half on the road, half on the pavement. By this time Beetle has climbed through too, and is now walking up and down the back seat howling; Titus alone, the plumpest of the three, remains in the cage, wailing in protest. In desperation I put the cage on the back seat and firmly shove Beetle and Fannie back inside it. I proceed with the journey, and in less than fifteen seconds Fannie reappears under my feet. I bend down and grab her by her scruff and lift her on to my lap where I hold her firmly with one hand and attempt to drive with the other. Eventually I reach my destination and take them into the vet's reception area. As I'm standing at the desk I realise that the front of both my thighs are seeping blood through my jeans where Fannie has repeatedly buried her claws into me in terror, but there is nothing to be done. We pass the time, noisily, as other people accompanied by their animals, waiting for their own appointments, coo obligingly at the kittens and I smile affably, while trying to ignore my smarting legs.

Our turn finally comes and we go in to see Pat. She confirms immediately that the squeaking Fannie is all girl, which I knew; and that the now silent Beetle is all boy, which I had expected. But she confounds me totally over Titus, whom she declares to be female. When I query it, she calls in someone else for a second opinion and they both confirm Titus is female. They admit it's hard to sex a kitten that young, but finally – on demonstration – I accept their diagnosis.

'Help, because she's now registered as Titus and it's a boy's name,' I agonise.

'Well, give me a girl's name then.'

'But she's so much Titus already.'

'Then that's fine. She is a female Titus. OK, Titus?' and she pats Titus affectionately; and so she is, and always will be, Titus.

All three of them are injected, resulting in varying degrees of protest. Fannie most, Titus least, and Beetle in between. They are otherwise declared to be in good health, and have all the bits that a healthy kitten requires.

With some dread, I contemplate the journey back home. The receptionist manages to find me a bin liner, which I gratefully tie over the cage – and although Fannie gets out of the cage and into the bin liner on the way home, at least she stays out of the footwell. As I arrive back at the cottage, I realise with a sickening sensation in the pit of my stomach that they could so easily have got out of the cage as I was carrying them across the main road. I drive the car on to the pavement immediately outside the cottage and bundle the black-covered cage firmly in through the front door.

Now that they have been injected, we face another crisis. The time is fast approaching for Eve and Jenny (and John and Matthew) to take delivery of Beetle. Eve has suggested a Friday, so that Jenny will have the treat of a whole weekend to bond with Beetle immediately following his arrival at his new home. Beetle is in fact a very lucky boy, for he is going to a home where he will be well loved and which must be close to cat-heaven. Eve and John live beside a nearby lock, where John is the lockkeeper, and their cottage is in the middle of open countryside and as far away from a main road as it's possible to be. Fields, woodland and huge gravel pit lakes surround them. The possibilities for hunting for little Beetle are just infinite. Also, in the cat world the boys in the family appear always to be sent away or choose to go away of their own volition, so Beetle, if left to his own devices in our household, would probably have upped sticks and moved away anyway even if we had kept him.

Knowing all of this, however, does not make the pain easier and I approach the Friday of his departure with melancholy. Eve and Jenny are coming round at 8 p.m., and I return from work so late on this particular day, the traffic out of London being at its horrendous Friday worst, that at the very moment I get back and slip the key into the lock they arrive, as arranged. I literally just have time to grab him and bundle him into their cat carrier and that is that.

After they have gone, I sit down and whisper behind the closed door: 'Goodbye, Beetle. Be a good boy and remember to write sometime.'

CHAPTER 20

I watch the two remaining sisters anxiously for any indication that they might be missing Beetle, but there is no discernible change in their behaviour that could be construed as pining. They play even more manically, if anything, than they did when there were three of them. When I ask Eve how Beetle has settled in, she reports that they have all been in stitches at his antics and that he is either at full tilt or flat out, fast asleep. He is still being kept inside, for the moment, as he has not yet had his second course of injections. The next time I see Eve, she laughingly says: 'We all think he's mad. Mad as a hatter – but completely gorgeous.'

As July advances, hot and dry for the most part, Septi still keeps his own counsel and spends the majority of his waking hours out in the garden and beyond. He comes into the cottage to eat and sometimes to sleep, but he is back on his lone patrols. I suspect he continues to mourn Otto.

By this time we have, with much sadness, made the very hard decision to keep the kittens confined within the cottage as the main road outside is simply too treacherous. I talk to a friend, who is also a vet, and she shrugs, saying: 'I always feel you need to let cats take their chances outside, but I grant that a year is not much of a life-span. I do warn you, though, that if you keep them inside you must be firm at all times and not weaken, so they are used to the indoor life only. It must be one or the other.' I am in an agony of indecision, but Michael has no such qualms. 'Mo, let them go free and it's only a matter of how long. We *must* keep them inside. As long as we live in this house, you are going to have to get used to the idea.'

I do, however, spend many hours thinking about it, and trying to find a way round the problem. The garden is impossible to make cat proof and no cat understands that a standard garden fence should be considered to be its perimeter. I find a site on the Internet, which supplies cat-containment fencing, but it's American and they cannot send the materials to me because of the prodigious costs. For the moment I am beaten, and have to accept that the kittens will be interned.

Septi appears to relish his sole right of exeat and saunters out with his tail up, sometimes throwing an inscrutable glance over his shoulder as he sets off. The kittens watch him go, possibly bemused, but they do not especially show any sign of wishing to follow him. They are fully occupied by the distractions of their own making within the boundaries of the cottage itself.

Titus and Fannie have become inseparable. They sleep together, they fight together, they play together, they eat together, and they groom each other. They are developing rapidly and their eyes have changed from the baby-blue to what will be their adult colouring. Fannie, who is now a replica of her mother, has the same tiny, pointy, heart-shaped face and almond-shaped geisha stripes round her eyes. Her eye colour is more greeny than the striking amber of her mother's, but she is as near a clone as it's possible to imagine.

Titus is developing into a smaller version of her father, with dramatically large whiskers and a smiley mouth. Her ginger (or, more properly, red) coat is thick and fluffy and stripy throughout; she has a white bib with socks to match. Most arrestingly, she has dark golden eyes, the exact colour of her fur. Titus is more easy-going and languorous than Fannie, and lies on her back and schmoozes with one and all. She's especially fond of John and spends as much time with him as possible. He spends a lot of time lying still watching television and Titus likes that. It means she can lie on him, also being still and watching television. She eats more than Fannie and has a tiny potbelly.

Fannie is a much fussier eater and has a tendency to have a bit of this, and a bit of that. Mostly she likes to eat Septi's food when he is there, and surprisingly he lets her do that. I find her heartbreakingly cute because she is so like her mother. She loves dripping taps, just as Otto did. She is very wary, quite nervous, and I suspect more intelligent than Titus – but this is just assumption. She licks my eyelids just before I am going to sleep, and always sleeps in our room. At night the kittens both find separate sleeping places, although they sleep curled up together during the daytime.

By the beginning of August, Septi's relationship with the kittens has changed very slightly and he now sometimes plays with them a little. One of the things that Michael and I find extraordinary about his play with the kittens, which was not the case when he played with Otto, is that he stops playing with them the moment he thinks we are watching him.

The powerful sense of dignity, which all cats possess, never ceases to impress me. Sometimes, although it never seems to last for very long, he will allow one or other of the kittens to lie in the armchair next to

him. If, however, both of them climb up to be with him then, invariably, he will grunt discouragingly in the manner of an old man and, rising stiffly, he will abandon his resting place and ask one of us to let him go outside to his private wide-open spaces. It's hard to determine whether Septi is indulging the kittens, whether he really likes them, or what he feels about them at all. I long for him to respond to them as he did to Otto, but that may be hoping for too much.

Halfway through August, John and Kathy and Delilah come to visit us once again. This is the first time since the kittens were born, and I am hoping for good things as the kittens are comparatively young, so surely they will be more adaptable. Wrong. Fannie is every bit her mother's daughter, and behaves equally disgracefully as Otto did, spitting neurotically at every turn at poor Delilah. Titus is much more phlegmatic and once or twice she and Delilah rub noses. We conclude that were Titus and Delilah to be left alone they would become the best of friends, but poor Fannie has a long distance to go yet awhiles.

Although Michael and I try to conceal which cat or

kitten might be our favourite at any one time, Damian has no doubts at all, and does not attempt to conceal it. Without any question, Fannie is his. Damian has now provided Fannie especially (Titus is not as interested) with a source of endless amusement. In early August he wins a large goldfish at a visiting local funfair, which mysteriously enters the cottage under the cover of darkness, and the first I know of this aquatic addition to our family is when I go searching for my large yellow pastry-making bowl and find it complete with fish, water and pebbles in Damian's bedroom. Disarmingly formally, he introduces his fish to me as 'Bertie'. I remember all too clearly how many fish I inflicted upon my own parents, for my mother to clean out on a weekly basis, to be able to make any remark other than, 'Er, welcome, Bertie.' Shortly after this, Damian invests in a sizeable fish tank complete with pump and lid to house Bertie more comfortably on a permanent basis, which provides all of us with a greater peace of mind.

Since the introduction of Bertie into our home, Fannie in particular has developed a special welcoming ceremony for him, which involves complicated gymnastics. Having persuaded Damian to allow her into his room (she is the only one allowed free access), she then jumps up on to the cupboard, which is the platform for Bertie's tank. The first part of her greeting is, very delicately but repeatedly, to pat the side of the tank with her paw. This always has an electric, and presumably from Fannie's perspective, desirable, effect on Bertie, who charges full tilt round the tank, making waves. This is now the cue for her to jump up higher on to the top of the bookcase, which stands on top of the cupboard, behind the tank. From there, she diligently studies Bertie, head turning from side to side, and then proceeds to hang down from above to get an even closer view of him and to see if there is the slightest chance that he might be persuaded to leave his watery cell and jump out and join her. She appears fascinated by him and watches him for huge amounts of time.

In late August Annie comes to visit us again and is enraptured by the kittens, as I knew she would be. We have another 'epic' night and in the morning, when all of us discover we are rather the worse for wear, I invite Annie who, because John and Damian are both at home, has been exiled to the sofa bed in the sitting room for the night, to use the sanctuary of our bedroom to dress and spruce herself up. As an echo of less than a year ago, when Otto was alive, Annie is playing with both Fannie and Titus in our bedroom, and yet again I hear that enchanting laughter of hers as she talks quietly to them both.

She has to go early as she has things she must do at home. Damian, with great courtesy, and somewhat to my surprise, offers to escort Annie home on the convoluted tube route she must take to get to her flat and, unknown to us, that is the last we are to see of Damian for many weeks, as it seems it's not Fannie alone who has won his heart.

CHAPTER 21

As summer fades into autumn, the kittens display increasing degrees of affection for, and dependence upon, the human members of the household, and we have to be especially careful when cuddling either one of them, as each of them betrays conspicuous symptoms of jealousy. This will vary from a plaintive but artless miaowing, while staring fixedly at the human who is currently indulging in feline disloyalty, usually demonstrated by Fannie, to a more complex turning of the back and constrained sighing and then walking off disdainfully if approached – the most commonly adopted stand-off used by Titus.

As our holiday approaches, I begin to experience pre-France anxieties. We have decided not to put them in a cattery, but even though John will be at the cottage, I'm fearful that they may think that we will not come back, which they have already experienced with their mother and their brother.

Eve has very sweetly agreed to come in once a day to feed and water all three of them. Only last weekend John forgot his duties – when we came back, the water bowls were dry, which has made me panic.

We have a wonderful holiday in Languedoc, although I miss the kittens terribly – and for much of the time I find also that I am haunted by memories of the beautiful Otto, and that she stays inside my head. Much to my relief, when we finally come home we find the cats in one piece and the kittens seem totally forgiving of our abandonment of them. They are touchingly affectionate, so I conclude being left on home ground is a better option by far than a cattery, and I feel guilty for having doubted John's efficiency.

Septi, on the other hand, seems especially out of sorts with us. He refuses to be stroked or cuddled, and for several days he walks off if either Michael or I go near him. We discover from both John and Eve that he has repeatedly emptied his bowels on the bathroom carpet and outside John's bedroom. Every night now I put down Puppy Training Pads; these have plastic backings and are impregnated with a chemical that attracts animals to make use of them in this way. Septi is generally accommodating enough to avail himself of them rather than the carpet. However, if I attempt to move them away from John's door, which remains his optimum site, he continues to perform there, so we have no option but to keep the Puppy Pad routine going outside that door. I have tried using a cat-litter tray instead, but he stubbornly performs outside it rather than in it. I have heard it said that once a cat starts refusing its cat-litter tray and uses other places, it's a sign of some disturbance, so I am concerned at what is upsetting the poor old boy.

As the weather heralds autumn by rattling at the cottage windows and doors with a series of rain-filled gales, flattening all the remaining perennials in the garden, Septi spends more and more time indoors, and with some relief I observe that now at last he does seem

to have established a rapport of sorts with the two girls. He seems to spend most time with Fannie; does he see her mother in her? She is the more obviously flirtatious of the two of them and will actively seek him out, in contrast to her laid-back sister who likes the world to come to her. And yet it's perhaps the laid-back nature in Titus that is at times more appealing to Septi as she is less threatening, and will lie comfortably still for hours at a time, gently purring. From time to time I find him lying on a sofa flanked by them both, but I have never seen him share with them the special companionably close proximity that he would enjoy with Otto.

Truth to tell, the things that might happen between them are not always seen by me, and catwise there may be much that goes on that I do not know. They are true to themselves and keep their own counsel.

Around this time I receive an email from my friend
Sue, who has for some months been in quiet mourning
at the loss of her adored Devon Rex cat Spottiswoode,
and who knows that the only long-term fix is to find
another Devon Rex.

From:	Sue
To:	Marilyn
Date:	Monday 8 November 1999 23:43

Dear Marilyn
  I went to see a Devon Rex kitten
today. I trailed all the way to a
place near Bedford - the nearest kitten
I could find.

He is a Si-Rex, so a Devon Rex with Blue Siamese points. At the moment he is eleven weeks old, and when he sits on his fat little bottom he fits in the palm of your hand. He is an outcross - his mother was a Burmese with a Rex father.

I am afraid to say I put a deposit down, and seeing him climbing up the curtains knew with dread just what I shall be letting myself in for at the end of the month.

God help me if they don't all get on, but there were four dogs in the house as well as various uncles, aunts, brothers and sisters, so hopefully he is pretty gregarious.

As I have Chatto and Cape it would make sense to have a Bodley Head, but this is not a good cat name, so I shall call him Max Reinhardt who, I believe, became part of Bodley Head through Putnam. Max Reinhardt used to publish one of my favourite British humorists - Paul Jennings - so I have always thought he must have been a good egg! He will only have to use his

surname on forms and tax returns, so
Max is a good cat name for everyday.
  Love Sue

Because I am lucky enough to have a car
and Sue does not, and because I am
a complete pushover for kitten collection,
I nag Sue into letting me drive her to
collect her new family member. She
has a lively time ahead of her, as she
will be introducing her new Devon
Rex into an established household
of three Siamese/Burmese females.
However, new kittens,
for the following
reasons and many others, are excellent
diversions for those in mourning.

So far we have:

- been in oven (once)
- fridge (twice)
- fallen off kitchen counter bottom first into bowl of Whiskas (great shock for Nora at the time) - unfortunately this did not coincide with fall in washing up bowl
- have stood on heater (not done this again)
- stood in saucepans on cooker countless times
- reprogrammed fax machine
- have ignored all nice toys and played endlessly with piece of blue parcel binding

However, we have made up for these transgressions by being very adorable and sleeping a lot, giving everyone a respite. Have even managed to sleep curled up with Jonathan, and Nora doesn't mind too much when we eat her dinner. Chatto was not impressed by the threat of loads more Maxes arriving, and at least is sulking a little less spectacularly. We do spoil things a bit by chancing our arm (or paw) just a little too often, and things have not got so friendly that tail chasing is acceptable as yet. Eating continues to be a favourite habit and we oblige by hoovering down everything and anything including other people's dinner – who, although tolerant, do not like having it stood in. I think you know to whom I refer.

Sue

My postscript to this is that Max Reinhardt is a knockout. He is so pretty and so naughty that he has hooked me totally on to the breed of Devon Rex.

We make a foray into Scotland with the kittens where we stay with Michael's brother, John, for a week. The week we are in Scotland is splendid, but the long journey is not a success and Michael's despair makes me ponder seriously on the wisdom of undertaking journeys in the car with two kittens. It is certainly a tax on a marriage, regardless of whether or not it is healthy for the kittens in question.

We return to the cottage in time to make all the myriad arrangements necessary for Christmas, and happily look forward to the company of Damian and John who will both share it with us. Sadly, Oliver must work, so we forgo the pleasure of his company and he remains in Wales with his mother.

Septi's 'problem', which has been a regular occurrence over the last few months, is currently in abeyance, so I'm hoping it might have 'gone away'. He continues to tolerate the kittens and even, sometimes, seems to enjoy their company, so perhaps his antisocial toilet activities were merely a temporary protest.

CHAPTER 22

December 1999

My former husband, Geoffrey, who is a close friend to us both, invites us to stay with him in the Yorkshire Dales. He has even extended the invitation to the kittens too. He has never been a cat lover, so I'm aware of the indulgence he is affording us. He lives in a large Georgian house in the Dales, which I shared with him for many years, and I can just imagine the pleasure with which Titus and Fannie will rampage around it. We load up the car and set off on our journey, as we did before on the Great Scottish Expedition.

It is a strange fact but the memory can be curiously selective in what it retains and what it rejects. Somehow the interval of Christmas has wiped the memory of the Scottish journey from our minds. But suddenly I have total recall.

As we turn in west from the A1 to wind our way up the valley of the Ure, following that great river that never flinched at any obstacle in its way as it evolved its riverbed, but rather twisted and turned a myriad times empowered by its never-ending supply of Pennine hill water, I realise that the resulting travel sickness from the kittens is absolutely inevitable and that I should have been able to predict that this is what would happen.

I feel my own pleasure at returning 'home' being inexorably diluted by Michael's increasing horror at the smell and inconvenience of stopping every five miles to clean up, and on this occasion I do know that his foreseeable 'No, this time I mean it. This *really* is the last time. Never, ever again' is a serious, to-be-forgotten-at-my-peril, warning.

We arrive at Park House in the dark and pull up at the back door. We are met by Geoffrey, who calls out to us with his customary greeting to all visitors who approach his manse from this angle, and which on all previous occasions has made us both giggle: 'Please MIND the dog shit. There's a lot of it about.'

He has a deep horror of visitors bringing in unwanted 'calling cards' on their shoes, having suffered a seminal experience of this nature some years earlier. The little ginnel at the back of the house is a favourite short-cut of dog walkers, and also solo dogs, that, Geoffrey is adamant, particularly favour the verge outside his Reading Room window as their chosen latrine. I cannot bear to tell him that we are one travelling car full of much worse than this. I creep round the side of the car and give him a big kiss and Michael comes up the other side of him and grips him in a bear hug, and then we hush him back inside the house. I then retrace my steps and try to pile all the detritus from our sickly journey into a bin liner, and then into his dustbin, without him being especially aware of what I'm up to.

It is a bitterly cold night and there is already a heavy frost lying outside, but inside the house it's as warm as toast. The central heating is at full pitch and I can see an enormous log fire burning in the grate in the sitting room. We gratefully sink into the welcoming luxury of the warm house and let the kittens out of their cage. They scamper around in a flurry of delight. Now, at last, no sickening car movement and loads of space to move and exciting new places to investigate; what more could two young healthy cats possibly want?

Geoffrey makes some modest requests about places he would rather they did not visit, which I try to enforce, but that turns out to be more difficult than I had foreseen. Mealtimes prove to be the main stumbling block as that is when the kittens are most used to being with us. I am, however, much moved by Geoffrey's growing enchantment with them. He has always had a fondness for dogs and he and I both loved, and were loved in return, by our yellow labrador, Sam, some years earlier; but in common with many dog lovers who have not known cats closely, he has also always claimed that he does not like cats. They are selfish, scratchy and unreliable creatures in his view.

Dog-love is awesome for the recipient of it, who is given, regardless of whether they seek it or not, the most unselfish and unconditional loving they will ever encounter, and I found myself that this background ill prepares the hitherto dog-only person for the world of cats, and the love of cats, and the stoicism of cats, and the loyalty of cats – and the stubbornness of cats. And also for the courage of cats, and the elegance of cats and the humour of cats, and that these things are distinct and special to the species. All of which I'm trying to tell him now. But it's enough that for this moment he is watching Fannie and Titus with amusement and evident pleasure. They are responsive cats, and he is rewarded for his attentions to them by small gestures of affection in their typically brief, catlike way. He is also charmed by Fannie's delicate, girly, tiptoeing around the place, and Titus's more in-your-face approach of turning over on her back waiting for her tummy to be rubbed, or simply just climbing on to his knees regardless.

All in all, as always when returning to Geoffrey in Gayle, it's a tremendously enjoyable visit. Michael and I visit nearby friends, Kath and John and Doreen and Thomas, who are mildly bemused that we are indoctrinating cat lore into Park House, but all of them are cat lovers anyway, so they understand our madness.

When we take our leave, Geoffrey very generously invites the girls back again, but I know, even without discussion with Michael, that they have been allowed their last excursion, as they are such terrible travellers.

The journey home is not a good one. There has been a major pile-up on the M1 south of the point at which we join it, and we find ourselves trapped, stationary, for several hours and eventually, breaking all rules, the only way we can cope with the protesting prisoners is to let them have the run of the car until the police are able to clear the road and traffic is able to move freely again. It is the final seal on the end of journeying.

CHAPTER 23

The New Millennium – the year 2000

We arrive back at Moon Cottage in time for New Year's Eve and all its attendant revelry. Although we have so far resisted the extraordinary hype surrounding this occasion, both on the day and then the night itself, Michael and I, along with thousands of others, find ourselves enormously moved by the truly global nature of the televised celebrations. We watch, rapt, as New Zealand and Australia, and then China and India, see in the New Millennium. In the late evening we walk down to our local church and find that although there is no formal service underway, about fifteen local people have turned out to silently pray in the New Year; and as the midnight hour arrives, there is an enormous whoosh as nearby fireworks are let off to celebrate the moment, and the darkened windows of the church are lit up by the lurid greens and pinks of rockets and catherine wheels and we hear the distant sound of laughter and applause.

We leave the church, greeting our fellow parishioners as we go, and then start our walk home through the streets. We suddenly find ourselves and others calling out and greeting one another with true warmth and friendship and it does seem a very special moment.

As we near the cottage the sky is lit up all around us, again and again, by the multiple dazzle of fireworks, and the air is filled with repeated explosions of variable loudness. We look at each other and speed up our walking pace, aware too late of the effect that this hubbub will be having on Septi. We put the key in the door and call him, but we are unable to find him. Fannie, followed shortly by Titus, comes forward to greet us and they both appear untroubled by the general commotion, but we cannot track down Septi. In due course, we uncover him crouching on the seat of a dining room chair, under the overhang of a tablecloth. His eyes are large and he looks unhappy. There is a discernible 'frown' on his forehead and his cheek pads are puffed out, making his whiskers bristle. His ears lie alternately flat against his head or bolt upright, and his nostrils are quivering.

'Oh Septi – it's all right, boy. I promise you it's OK. They won't hurt you.' Michael holds him in his arms, and I come across to stroke him too. 'If I could stop the beastly things, Septi, I would,' I murmur.

It has been a matter of concern to me that, certainly for the last two years and possibly longer, in a neighbouring street to ours, we have been aware of fireworks not just on 5 November, which is when they might normally be expected to be heard, but now regularly on other occasions. The winning of local football, birthdays, anniversaries, who knows what might be the reason, but now there seems to be no closed season to when they might happen. Fireworks have an awful effect on some, although not all, animals, and I would love those who use them regularly to have more awareness of how much distress they may be causing. However, having said this, I can see that the dawn of the New Year of a New Millennium might reasonably be considered to be something worth celebrating in this manner.

Michael and the boys have no knowledge of what it was that happened in Septi's youth that so frightened him, but maybe, once, he was too close to a firework as it exploded and he has never forgotten the horror of it. Is it possible, on the other hand, that some cats and dogs, and also some horses, cattle and sheep – not to mention hundreds of other small mammals and most birds – are just simply terrified of these harmful-sounding detonations, and that they may never be able to conquer their fear of them?

~

Spring arrives, and with it a discernible difference in the girls now. They are beginning to develop and become very 'teenaged'. Fannie, who is more and more girly all the time, and usually extraordinarily delicate in where she places her feet, or where she lies, has suddenly started to break things.

As I walk into the room early this evening I'm just in time to see her knock over my desk light and smash the light bulb. As I watch this performance with my jaw agape, she then proceeds, right in front of me, to knock over the printer and thereby pull out all the cables. She has phases of racing round as if 'Old Nick' is after her, or more accurately, as if she is after 'Old Nick'.

Titus watches her excesses with a seemingly more adult disdain, but I wonder if it's not that Titus eats more, and is carrying more weight, so simply cannot be bothered to do the running. However, the two of them do continue, regularly, to play tag with each other and they seem on this one to take it turn and turn about. It starts downstairs, it involves heavy pounding up the stairs, running the full length of the upper

corridor, round and under John's bed, back into our room, up and over and behind our bed, and back down the stairs again. It is quite extraordinarily noisy, and at the end of it they are both quite breathless.

Fannie has also started to fish for Bertie with both her front legs in the water at the same time, if the lid is left off the fish tank. She sometimes squats on the top of the tank on her back legs and puts her front legs down into the water by pure balance. It's nerve-racking to watch from outside the tank, and must be terrible for Bertie, so it has to be stopped, although she is never anywhere near catching him in truth.

Titus definitely prefers men and when there is a choice of bodies will always select a man to lie on. Women are favoured only by default. Being red-haired she especially likes dark suits. Navy blue and black are best, so she can really leave her mark. She quietly climbs on to the knee of any and every man who visits the house and, given time, will slowly and insidiously climb up their shoulder, and then sit, nestled in the crook of the arm, leaning her own head against the human cheek of her choosing, purring quietly. At this moment John is her number one man, with Michael a very close second.

Fannie prefers to lie next to people rather than on them, and will usually choose me, or Damian if he's around. Her special thing with me is to wait outside the bathroom in the morning when she hears me running the shower, and when at the end I open the bathroom door she leaps in and jumps on to my knee for her morning cuddle, which is now highly ritualised. Truth to tell, I get so much peace and tranquillity out of those few moments of schmoozing before work that I could hardly bear it were it to cease. No wonder hospital patients find the company of animals healing.

Septi's toilet problems throughout this time continue and we all learn to live with stepping over the soiled Puppy Pads outside John's room on the upstairs landing, although it is of course much worse for John than for the rest of us.

On Saturday 1 April, the semi-final of the FA Cup is to be played at Wembley between Aston Villa and Bolton Wanderers, the latter being significant as the team that Geoffrey, as a son of Bolton, supports. As a consequence, Michael and Geoffrey, without much involvement on my part, engineer the purchase of a pair of tickets and Geoffrey comes to stay with us for the weekend. Knowing, of old, Geoffrey's distaste for all things associated with animal incontinence, I look forward to the weekend with minor apprehension on the cat front, but with the exception of one slight 'hiccup', and by the stealth of my early rising to destroy the evidence, Septi gets away with it.

It says much for Geoffrey's new-found affection for the kittens that in spite of the fact that Bolton gets beaten on the penalty shoot out, he is able to return to the cottage with Michael and be buoyant enough to announce that they are the only cats he has ever actively liked. Truth is, I think they are the first cats he has actively had inflicted upon him.

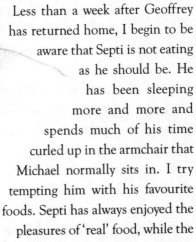

Less than a week after Geoffrey has returned home, I begin to be aware that Septi is not eating as he should be. He has been sleeping more and more and spends much of his time curled up in the armchair that Michael normally sits in. I try tempting him with his favourite foods. Septi has always enjoyed the pleasures of 'real' food, while the kittens have become addicted to Hill's Science Plan dried cat food and cannot be persuaded to eat anything else, except for a shared pack once a day of Friskies Go-

Cat wet cat food. Septi, on the other hand, eats sardines, ham, salmon, prawns and pretty much any brand of proprietary cat food as long as it's wet; he does not like dried food.

During this period he responds initially to salmon, and then to some ham, but very soon he leaves even these delicacies. I have begun to watch him closely, and twice have seen him turn round and, as he has moved, he has made a small, almost inaudible, moaning sound. I am worried, but do not want to say anything to Michael yet.

Eventually, though, I say: 'Michael, I think the old boy is in pain. I have been watching him and he is groaning when he moves – and you know Septi, he's a real stoic.'

'Are you sure? No – you're fine, aren't you, boy?' Michael strokes him gently. He then, with both hands, puts gentle pressure on either side of Septi's ribcage, and at that we both hear the old cat groan, which he follows with a long sigh. I see a sad look pass across Michael's face like a dark cloud, and I feel a double stab of pain, for him and for Septi.

I find suffering in animals harder to bear than in adult humans. I imagine it's similar to the feeling that parents have when they see their child in hospital, frightened and in pain. It engenders an overwhelming sense of helplessness at not being able to explain it, or alleviate it.

The following day finds me setting off in the car with, unusually, Septi in the cat carrier. Having not taken him to the vet for a long time I am not sure what to expect, and am much saddened by his outraged howls of protest and fear, which he keeps up all the way to the surgery.

On this first visit we see James, who is clearly worried by Septi's condition, but initially gives me antibiotics to clear up any infection that might be causing the problem. When I get Septi back home, he does eat a bit initially, so I hope against hope that this has sorted out his problem. Soon afterwards, though, he stops eating again and it is very clear that he is having trouble with his stomach.

We return, yet again, to the vet and once more see James. He handles Septi with great care and gentleness, and very thoroughly checks him out all over.

'Tell me again exactly how old this cat is.'

'He's either nineteen or twenty, we're not sure.'

'He has had a very good innings, you know.'

I wait, braced.

James looks at me. I know he is trying to see what he should say. It's hard being a vet, because you have to handle people, as well as their animals.

I look back at him and murmur: 'Go on. Say it.'

'You know what I'm going to say, I think. I believe that your cat has tumours and they seem to me to be pretty widespread, but . . .,' he says, as he sees my eyes fill with tears, 'I believe that he still has some quality of life ahead of him, and there is something we can do to help him as a temporary measure. Are you prepared to give it a go?'

I nod bleakly.

He rummages around in the huge drawer behind him, while I fondle Septi helplessly, and he then produces the inevitable syringe and injects Septi with a huge dose of steroids.

'You must understand that this will not cure him, but what I hope it will do is give him a new lease of life, and it may restore his appetite. I have given him a very large dose of steroids, but cats are surprisingly tolerant of them. You will be able to tell within the next seventy-two hours whether it's doing any good or not.'

When I break the news to John and Michael after returning home from that second visit, they are wretched beyond description, and I cannot find the words that will help them. Loving animals exacts its toll in pain at their weakness.

By the following day, however, Septi is eating like we cannot remember seeing him eat in years. He eats chicken, fish, and even some ham, and would, I believe, eat all manner of food if we gave him the chance.

Michael, always the optimist, keeps grinning as we watch Septi eating yet another plate full of food, and says he knows it's a miracle and that Septi will be all right after all. Oh, I so want this to be true. Certainly the old cat's eyes have a sparkle in them and it's the first time in days that he has eaten without being sick. It does appear as if his pain has been alleviated in some way.

James, during my last visit, had warned me, however, that when Septi next slips 'down' they will not be able to help me further, and that I will know instinctively when the right time to 'take action' will be. I am not so sure.

From:	Marilyn
To:	Sue
Date:	13 April 2000 17:08

On Septi, don't think he has long now and the awful bit is don't know how or when to do the dreaded end bit.

Michael is distraught because he has had him man and boy (Septi is twenty and Michael has had him since a kitten).

Marilyn

Oh how dreadful. Having lost Spotty at nineteen years, I have some idea of how awful all this is.

Charlotte, my first cat, had cancer, and we called it a day as soon as she started sitting hunched up and not eating, but you are left with that dreadful thought of should I? It is horrible to have to play God, but I did feel better that I got the vet to come to her and do it, and held her at the end, so the slip from life to death was as painless for her as possible. So, if it comes to it, do insist the vet comes to you.

In great sympathy
Sue

Septi continues for a short time to gain strength from his new voracious eating, but now he has stopped eating chicken and ordinary fish. He will only eat cold ham and hot bacon, which is strange food – but pork clearly has what it takes for him. He is painfully thin in spite of his bingeing, but he still walks around the house and goes outside to do the all-important things that a cat has to do.

He seems to me, and Michael and John, fantastically brave. We are sure he must be in pain, but his courage is phenomenal. He lies alternately on the sofa and on the chair, and the kittens, although they come close to him from time to time, are keeping what seems like a respectful distance. They walk around the room and look up at him, but they do not jump up next to him.

I notice how both John and Michael take time to talk to Septi gently and I ache for them. I, too, when they are not around, find myself talking to him more than I ever did in the past, as Septi was always so much his own cat that somehow it would have been impertinent before.

As he loses more weight and sleeps for an increasing amount of time, I talk to Michael about what I should do about the vet. He makes a joke about Septi being a Catholic cat, and as such cannot be subjected to euthanasia. My eyes fill with tears, as I hug my man, who is simply in denial at the fact that Septi might be dying. However, joke though it is, it doesn't make it any easier to decide when or how.

CHAPTER 24

Septi barely moves from either the sofa or Michael's leather armchair. He has stopped eating, although he is still drinking a small amount of water. Hitherto, as he has been sleeping he has mostly been facing into the room, but I have noticed that now he lies with his back curled away from the room, and my father, a physician, always said that when a patient's head is turned permanently to the wall, it is of significance.

On the Wednesday before Easter I drive down to the West Country to see Paul and Sue, and when I get back that night Septi does not move. I know the moment is now. The Easter weekend is approaching and vets will be hard to get hold of, and I cannot abide to see him suffering any longer. It is truly unbearable.

Michael and I talk that evening and I know now that Michael cannot tolerate it any longer either. We both know that Septi will die anyway, whatever we do.

The following day Michael and John both leave to go to their offices and I'm upstairs when John leaves, so do not hear him say his farewell to Septi, but I know that he does and guess how much it hurts him. As Michael is about to leave, I'm not brave enough to be in the room when he says his goodbye to Septi, but shortly afterwards I hear his sob even from the room where I'm hiding. I go out to him and his desolation shatters me.

After they have left the cottage, it goes deadly quiet. I beg Septi to forgive me, but know that I am asking too much all the same. As soon as the vet's surgery is open, I phone them and ask them to send a vet to the cottage and explain the reason for the home visit. They ask me if I am sure it's necessary and I reply rather crossly: 'Yes. I'm absolutely certain.'

'A vet will be with you, hopefully within the next two hours.'

That should make it 11 a.m.

It's a terrible day. I keep going in to look at Septi and am fearful that he will feel bad vibes from me and know what is in my evil mind.

At 1 p.m. I phone the surgery again and am told that the vet has had a very full morning of emergency calls, etc.

At 2.30 I call again. Still no news of when the vet will arrive.

At 3.15 the doorbell rings and I find myself facing the vet, who is standing on the doorstep, bag in hand. By this time, I find it hard to speak. She is kind and apologetic, and says she has had a nightmare of a day, including just despatching the victim, a large dog, of an especially grisly road accident.

I introduce her to Septi who ignores her and remains steadfastly in his chair with his back to her. She asks if it should be that chair and I say yes, and shut the kittens out of the room.

She opens her bag and assembles her equipment and

does the deed there and then, with gentleness and speed, but sadly the needle in the vein in his leg hurts him and he cries out and tries to move away. I hurt for him myself. She tries to hold him still, and I move across to be with him too. She injects him again. As I sit with him, with my hand on his side, his breathing stops.

The old warrior, the feisty one, is dead.

I have prepared a box with a sheet which I want to lay him out on, and I get up in order to fetch it from the adjoining room so that I might carry him away before the kittens see him.

'No, no. You must not do that,' she says. 'It's very important that they see him and understand that he is dead, otherwise they will not grieve and that is bad for them. Put him in the box, and then call them and let them smell him.'

We put him in the box and I do not cover him with the sheet; we call Fannie and Titus. They come to the box, gently, curiously. They both walk round to his head and smell his ears, his eyes and his nose. They look at each other and then they walk away, seemingly curiously detached, but also of one mind.

The vet and I talk for a while and I'm very grateful for her sympathy and understanding. She takes her leave and, after she has gone, I wrap Septi in the sheet and carry him in his box out to the greenhouse where I lay him with a candle at each end to await Michael's return. I know that he's going to be upset by the candles, but I also know that if I do *not* do this he will be upset anyway.

We say prayers for Septi and bury him under the pear tree. Michael then confesses to me: 'Today is the first day in all the time we have been together when I didn't want to come home. I knew, all day long, that when I finally got home, Septi wouldn't be there any more.'

He then says that finding the candles next to Septi helped him in some way. I know exactly what he means, and I owe this one to my wise friend Sue. When my dog, Sam, who contracted an awful kidney infection, was finally put down, I made the mistake of leaving his body with the vet for him to incinerate, and my last image of Sam was of his body being dragged across a cobbled yard in a bin liner. (Although in fact that is also the last image I had of my mother, not being dragged across the cobbles of course, but the undertakers took her body out of our house in a black body bag which looked just like a bin liner, and I had to make sure that my poor father, who was distraught in his grief, did not see her passing his study window looking like that.)

From:	Sue
To:	Marilyn
Date:	15 April 2000 22:57

I wish people [who don't have close companion animals] could sympathise more when you lose one. They, the animal, give so much for so little and it is impossible to describe what a gap they leave behind them when they go. I don't know if I should add this bit or not, but when Spotty died I felt awful that I only had an old box to put him in, and I did feel better after going out and buying a new cardboard

cat carrier to take him to the vets. I
laid him on a fresh pillow and gave him
some flowers, which made me feel a lot
better - why, I don't know, but it did.
  Best wishes,
  Sue

So not only has Sue helped on the matter of the final
vet visit to Septi, but also in providing him with dignity
in his death. Very sadly, a little later I then receive this
email from her:

From:	Sue
To:	Marilyn
Date:	31 May 2000 22:02

Just to let you know that I have also
now lost my 'old stager'. Poor old
Nora was going down hill rapidly, and
last week I took her to the vet one
last time. I was much luckier than you
as he did use the sedation routine and
left me with her while she fell asleep,
and then he gave her the last injection

so she didn't have to struggle like poor old Septi. I was quite touched by his consideration, and he even suggested I moved so that she could see me as she faded away. I knew it was coming so it didn't come as a complete blow, but it is always hard when you walk home with that empty basket.

It has been strange without her, the others don't seem to miss her as such, but their pattern of life has changed – and she was obviously keeping the peace with Max as he has got bashed more than ever without her here.

Life goes on . . .

Sue

Immediately after Septi's death the kittens are very strange indeed. For about three nights they have been leaping out of corners and rampaging around the house. Michael and John have both commented on it. Some of their behaviour is a knowledge that Septi is not here any more, I'm sure of it, and a letting-off of steam as they seemed to be on their 'best' behaviour while he was ill. Some of it, however, is uncomfortably to me as if they are seeing something the rest of us are not seeing? Animal grief remains a mystery.

I write an email to my friend Harriet, who has two sons, Josh and Robbie, saying that I still feel terrible guilt for betraying Septi's trust in me, and that on top of that the kittens are behaving very oddly and rushing around and running away. She replies:

From:	Harriet
To:	Marilyn
Date:	27 April 2000 22:27

Dearest M

So sorry to hear about Septi, but I think you misjudge that cat. I think he did trust you to the end to help him make that last leg of his journey, and who are we to suppose that what comes after death is not to be trusted. But sad to see him go. And I'm not surprised the kittens are flexing their newfound independence - they have a whole lot of additional space to occupy now. It is amazing how, when the status quo

changes, adjustments are made. You
should see Robbie, with Josh away,
expand in personality to take up the
slack in his brother's absence.
  Love Harriet

At the end of *Charles: The Story of a Friendship* by
Michael Joseph, a wonderful book about the special
relationship Michael Joseph had with his Siamese cat,
Charles, through the war years, he quotes Carl Van
Vechten writing about *his* cat, Feathers:

It is seemingly very simple, such a companionship, depending on scarcely more than mere
propinquity, a few actions, a touch of the
cold, moist nose, a soft paw against the cheek,
a greeting at the door, a few moments of
romping, a warm, soft ball of fur curled on the
knee, or a long stare. It is thus that the sympathy
between men and animals expresses itself, but
interwoven, and collectively, these details create

an emotion which it is very difficult even for time to destroy.[6]

And borrowing Michael Joseph's own tribute to his beloved Charles, may I say to both Otto and Septi, from all of us who loved them:

For while we live you shall not die.

---

[6] Taken from *Charles: The Story of a Friendship* by Michael Joseph (Michael Joseph, 1945).

ACKNOWLEDGEMENTS

Warmest thanks to Sue Baker, Annie Brumsen, Jane Cholmeley, Elspeth Dougall, Margot Edwards, Susan Hill, Caroline Michel and Dr Desmond Morris who have all, in various ways, helped me in the writing of this book.

And to my editor, Judith Longman, who has initiated me by the gentlest of coercion combined with an endearing enthusiasm into the rite of first-time publication, and also to all her colleagues within Hodder & Stoughton for their splendid support of this project.

To the artist Peter Warner, who as I write this is so magnificently decorating this book.

To Damian, Oliver and especially John, who are in it and part of it and to whom the cats and I owe a great deal.

To dear Michael, who has lived it, eaten it and slept it for far too long and without whom, most truly, it would not have happened.

And a special word of thanks to Geoffrey Moorhouse and to Giles Gordon, from whom I drew inspiration because they believed in it, encouraged me and fortified my resolve to continue. To find myself, even on so short a journey, a fellow traveller of two such writers moves me beyond words.

Animal **Health** Trust

Registered Charity 209642

The Feline Unit at the Animal Health Trust

Cats are now the most popular domestic pet in the UK. Although our knowledge of feline diseases has increased over recent years, our level of understanding of many of these conditions is still relatively poor. The Animal Health Trust is an internationally renowned centre of excellence that seeks to improve the health and welfare of animals by studying the diseases that affect them so that better diagnosis, treatment, control and prevention can be achieved. The Feline Unit provides a full clinical referral service for cats with internal medical diseases, and is a part of the small animal hospital at the Trust. It is dedicated to promoting feline welfare by providing the highest quality of care for sick cats, and by contributing to studies that are concerned with broader aspects of feline health and welfare that can impact on the quality of life of all cats.

The contact details for the Feline Unit at the Animal Health Trust are:

Lanwades Park
Kentford
Newmarket
Suffolk CB8 7UU
UK

Tel: (44) 8700 502424
Fax: (44) 8700 502425

Dr Andy Sparkes BVetMed, PhD, DipECVIM, MRCVS
RCVS Specialist in Feline Medicine
Head of the Feline Unit, the Animal Health Trust